UNREPORTED

UNREPORTED

Kaley Roberts

NEW DEGREE PRESS

COPYRIGHT © 2021 KALEY ROBERTS

UNREPORTED

ISBN

978-1-63676-907-3   *Paperback*

978-1-63676-971-4   *Kindle Ebook*

978-1-63730-075-6   *Digital Ebook*

For front porch revolutionaries everywhere and especially for those who appear in these pages.

Contents

"You may not control all the events that happen to you, but you can decide not to be reduced by them."

—MAYA ANGELOU

Introduction

———

At fourteen years old, Isla had priorities.

The new decade moved around her so quickly she knew it only by headlines. Obama began his second presidential year, the Saints won the Super Bowl, and Apple released a hot new device called the iPad (no one was really sure why they needed it, but they needed it anyway). *Lost*'s TV finale disappointed fans, *The Hunger Games* premiere wowed them, and when the credits rolled on both, people rushed to turn their phones back on (they had *Angry Birds* levels to complete). Wall Street was getting back on its feet, Miley and Liam were getting together, Julian Assange was getting torn apart, and it was all happening to the tune of Katy Perry's summer anthem, "California Gurls."

That bubblegum-pink, Candy Land, floating-on-a-cloud beat.

Isla was a sun-kissed freshman at Santa Monica High School with a wide smile and parents who worked in television—the stereotypical California girl. The oldest of five, she had strict rules by Los Angeles standards: no staying at parties past midnight, no getting into cars with people you don't know, no smoking weed. For a city kid, she was basically sheltered. And, like any firstborn fourteen-year-old, her main priority was to become less so.

Isla was raped that summer. A neighbor—who lived just houses down from her parents—assaulted her, taking her virginity and, with it, years of growing up slowly. We'll get into the details later. For now, all you need to know is Isla decided not to report. And, despite how alone she may have felt that night and for many, many nights after, she has sisterhood in her decision not to report.

Inadvertently, Isla joined a vast and quiet community that summer: the unreported.

SEVENTY-THREE SECONDS

A minute and thirteen seconds is enough time to speed-read the prologue of this book (maybe). It was enough time for Isla to exchange a few life-altering Facebook messages on her iPhone 4 during that night in 2010. It's enough time to get small things done but, ultimately, it is still just seventy-three seconds. No time at all.

Every seventy-three seconds, another story like Isla's begins spinning. Every seventy-three seconds, an American is sexually assaulted.[1]

An American life averages out at over twenty-two million seconds—lucky us. During that span, which can feel long or short depending on how you live it, one in five women is raped. One in seventy-one men is raped. The problem is pervasive, and that's speaking generally: specific populations, like Native American women and the LGBQT+ community, are at an even higher risk.[2][3]

1   "Statistics," RAINN (Rape, Abuse & Incest National Network), accessed February 19, 2021.

2   Matthew J. Breiding, Sharon G. Smith, Kathleen C. Basile, Mikel L. Walters, Jieru Chen, and Melissa T. Merrick, *Prevalence and Characteristics of Sexual Violence, Stalking, and Intimate Partner Violence Victimization—National Intimate Partner and Sexual Violence Survey,* United States, 2011 (Atlanta, Georgia: CDC, 2014).

3   "Sexual Assault and the LGBTQ Community," Human Rights Campaign, accessed February 19, 2021.

Sexual violence is an enigma. Despite its widespread nature, it somehow remains a unique and personal crime. The violence makes it personal. The violation: the unapologetic invasion of another body. As human beings, our bodies are our first and final home. Rape desecrates that shelter, trespassing in its most vulnerable places, hurting the deepest core. The memory of the assault—how it took power away the moment it happened and took peace for many moments after—becomes an intensely singular chapter in a person's story. No two excerpts look the same.

Something similar can be said for a slew of different crimes though: burglary, arson, nonsexual assault. They are often random, personal attacks, and the aftermath varies. So, while the violation makes it personal, it doesn't make sexual violence unique. That uniqueness is tied to sex.

We are born to know sex. Best-case scenario, we're born to like it. Add violence to the mix and you've paired a private, positive necessity with an obscene, unnecessary act. The juxtaposition makes sexual violence a challenge unlike any other.

Society knows sex. We understand crime. So, when it comes to sex as a crime, it's natural that we'd make a few assumptions. Among the top of the list of those assumptions?

If it were you, you'd report. It may not be easy, but you'd do it. Let's start there.

ASS-U-ME-ING

Only 25 percent of all sexual violence is reported to police, making it the most underreported crime.[4] [5] Isla was part of the 75 percent. The vast majority, the unreported. But if it were you…

---

4   "The Criminal Justice System: Statistics," RAINN (Rape, Abuse & Incest National Network), accessed February 19, 2021.

5   "Statistics About Sexual Violence," National Sexual Violence Resource Center, accessed February 19, 2021.

And then, it *is* you. You might be older or wiser or less vulnerable than Isla, but one night someone decides not to listen to you or decides not to ask. And with that single unwanted sexual act, you become some version of Isla. Suddenly, reporting doesn't feel so simple. Suddenly, a few things become clear.

First: sexual violence is bigger than injustice. It's injury. And while the cure for injustice could be justice, the antidote for injury is healing. Because of our natural instinct to survive, we move to mend the wound first. Stop the bleeding. As for the person who caused the pain? Holding them accountable is secondary—only after the injury has been bandaged does it become physically possible to do anything else. But then, even when you're able to move toward justice, a second assumption is called into question.

If it were you, you'd want justice. No doubt about it.

We all know about crime and punishment. In other cases, it means return the possessions. Repay the money. Do the time. But sexual violence? No amount of justice can erase that intensely personal chapter from your life once it's written. Nothing can make it fair now that your life has been irrevocably changed.

Some people find healing in justice. If the goal is to transform the hurt, restore the faith, and make the most of an altered story, then punishment can play a role. Getting justice can be an important part of a person's healing process. But that lands us at the third and final assumption.

If you were to seek justice, you'd find it.

In a world where reporting sexual violence has a non-negligible track record, maybe things are different. Perhaps people do go to authorities if there's a real chance that by doing so they can prevent the same perpetrator from acting again. But that is not our world. Instead of signaling safety or justice, our statistics spell out how the odds are—quite plainly—stacked against the assaulted. Only five perpetrators are convicted for every one thousand sexual assaults. For context, a little more than one in fifty criminals are convicted after a robbery.[6] In nonnumerical terms, that means the people perpetuating one of our nation's most rampant issues, which permeates society on so many levels, are not being punished.

Our system is failing. But the real problem? Everyone knows.

WHY DIDN'T I REPORT?

Christine Blasey knew. In 1982, before she became a doctor, before she added "Ford" to her last name, before she graduated from three universities with psychology degrees and became a professor at Stanford. Before even receiving her high school diploma, she knew. After a teenage boy assaulted her at a party, she joined the same sisterhood Isla would decades later: the unreported. She understood the majority consensus, and she rejected the failing system.[7]

Thirty-six years later, that failing system was put on trial and, remarkably, it won. The grown-up version of her boy assailant was appointed to the US Supreme Court, despite Dr. Blasey Ford's allegations against him. But no one questioned the system, or whether it was broken.

Instead, loud press coverage and dinner-table talk asked a different question. It echoed across our country, in a chorus of doubt. Many Americans spoke openly about how they *would* believe Dr. Blasey Ford, but there was one thing they

6   "The Criminal Justice System: Statistics," RAINN (Rape, Abuse & Incest National Network), accessed February 19, 2021.

7   The New York Times, "Read Christine Blasey Ford's Prepared Statement," *New York Times*, September 26, 2018.

didn't understand. One part of the story just did not make any sense to them. They asked the question that the former US President implied on Twitter.

"I have no doubt that, if the attack on Dr. Ford was as bad as she says, charges would have either been immediately filed with local Law Enforcement," his tweet began. "I ask that she bring those filings forward so that we can learn date, time, and place!"[8]

Why didn't she report?

I knew that question. I'd been asking it for years. Except it wasn't, *Why didn't she report?* It was, *Why didn't I?*

When I was violated, reporting did not feel like an option. It seemed there was only one way forward, and it was entirely about grasping to keep my life, which felt upended, as normal as possible. I spent the summer after the assault quietly processing, understanding what it meant that my "no" was disregarded, and what that would mean going forward. I bandaged the wound, stopped the bleeding. I journaled. I discussed it every Wednesday with my therapist. I moved West. And then coverage of Dr. Blasey Ford and her assailant blared throughout the nation.

I became furiously curious. I had just started working in the entertainment industry, where I encountered men who were older and less drunk than the guy from my freshman year of college, but just as heinous. Between production meetings, they didn't mention Dr. Blasey Ford. More often, they poked holes in other #MeToo headlines, asking that same sticky question of celebrities: *Why didn't she report?*

Away from the office, I spoke with friends about their experiences and interviewed others. I asked the question

---

8   Donald J. Trump (@RealDonaldTrump), "I have no doubt that…,"
     Twitter, September 21, 2018.

over and over again—*Why didn't you report?* I broke it down and decided to answer it for our forty-fifth president, for my colleagues, for the entire nation of people who asked Dr. Blasey Ford.

And for that hurt nineteen-year-old girl. My younger self.

I remembered how she woke up the next morning in a dorm with three friends. Alone. How deeply she craved healing and how the process of reporting seemed so contradictory to that desire. How she wrestled first with her decision not to report and then with the guilt of choosing not to. Especially after she learned the unpleasant truth:

If a rapist isn't stopped, they will, on average, commit the crime five more times.[9] And while this is a book, not a research paper, that statistic tells a story. Reporting is a crucial component of ending sexual violence. It's the difference between one assault and six.

AN ANTIDOTE FOR LOSS AND INJURY

In the aftermath of sexual violence, you're painfully aware of what you've lost. For Isla: the opportunity to explore sex on her own terms, in her own time. For any version of her: control. The entire essence of rape is you don't get to choose whether another person touches you here or penetrates you there. They decide for you. And in that lack of choice, you lose.

After any loss, priorities differ. But as humans, we tend to seek a return to the norm. We need control to get there; the freedom to navigate loss on our own terms. Especially after it's been taken away by an assailant, the reinforced knowledge that we are decision makers in our own lives is key.

---

9   David Lisak and Paul M. Miller, "Repeat Rape and Multiple Offending among Undetected Rapists," *Violence and Victims* 17, no. 1, (February 2002).

Current sexual violence reporting systems don't procure justice—again, only five of every one thousand rapists are convicted.[10] Perhaps just as detrimental for healing, though, is the fact that the systems do not give control back to the people who desperately need it in that moment. Instead of risking more loss by participating in the system, people who have been assaulted and raped choose not to.

They go unreported.

And can you blame them?

Sexual violence is not just crime. It's injury. The system for ending it needs to be bigger than punishment. It needs to enhance healing. When we create the system that people want—the one that Isla, Dr. Blasey Ford, and that hurt nineteen-year-old needed—it will be one that starts by stopping the bleeding. One that supplies bandages, care, and most importantly, the control to repair life in your way, on your time. It will be a system that values recovery above all else. And then, it will become a system that works.

SPOILER ALERT

If you know someone who has experienced sexual violence—spoiler alert, you do—this book is for you. It's for people who are at risk of being assaulted and it's for those who are in positions to help them. It's for women and, perhaps just as crucially, it's for men. *Unreported* is for anyone looking to empathize and understand the most underreported and prevalent crime currently plaguing our society.

And this book is for all those who are looking to repair a broken system. Because, in the stories ahead, there are

---

10 "Statistics," RAINN (Rape, Abuse & Incest National Network), accessed February 19, 2021.

blueprints for a new way: plans for an encouraging, effective system. As I worked through my own unreport and listened to others, the sketches built themselves. It turns out, explaining *why she didn't report* makes it clear under what circumstances she would have.

Mostly, though, *Unreported* is for the people who have lived these stories themselves. The vast majority. You are brave and, in the next 210 pages, you are heard.

AN ANSWER

Unreported sexual violence, by its very nature, often lives suspended in the story of the person it happened to. Somewhere between the moment consent was ignored, and the way they courageously carried on after, the story exists largely unheard.

In the chapters ahead, six different women share that great untold story: why they didn't report and how life has looked since. We look at famous cases of those who did report and analyze how their trajectory differed. A lifelong advocate against sexual violence, a former Harvard therapist, and a renowned journalist share their expertise on how to improve reporting systems. Together, we propose a healing-centric system.

Ultimately, *Unreported* answers the question that our entire nation has repeatedly asked. The question that points to the heart of where our system fails.

Why didn't she report?

ALL THAT YOU'LL FIND

"Whatever you give a woman, she will make greater."

—WILLIAM GOLDING

I grew up in the arms of many women.

My dad's mom is compassionate and effusive and lives just on the other side of town. My mom's sister and their mom are both a two-minute bike ride away, up the hills of our beachy neighborhood. Niantic, Connecticut: named for the indigenous peoples who lived here first. It's only warm enough to stay outside five months of the year, but even winter days glow with the sun's reflection on the ocean bouncing off each small-town interaction.

My favorite interactions always came at night. When the sun set and the breeze picked up, carrying sea salt through the air, up the street, to our front porch. On especially sacred evenings, that breeze carried women too. Gathered between window screens on secondhand couches, my mom, aunt, and grandma would sink into laughter and opinions and each other. My sister, Kendall, and I collapsed on laps and, with someone's fingers in our hair, we'd listen as they bounced words around the space. Even when I was four and Kendall was two, when we understood next to none of the dialogue, we had a silent pact that we'd never interrupt and ask. The rhythm of their stories was too sweet, the thoroughness of their life updates too illuminating. We curled our bodies up against one of theirs and feigned sleep, hoping to stay forever.

Porch talks had their own cadence, unlike any other conversation I heard my mom have. She chatted all over the house, wireless landline pressed between her shoulder and ear as she watered window boxes or repotted our new cactus. She stopped neighbors in the street, exchanging words while our dog pulled his leash. At Stop & Shop, she'd swing the cart around when she recognized someone turning an aisle. Kendall and I would groan. We wanted to get the errands over with, already. But also, mid-grocery dialogues were nothing like the porch talk we loved.

On the porch, words were honest and robust. Conversations there existed on a different plane than the way they sounded in town, on the landline, and basically everywhere else. The front-porch talks weren't necessarily more complex. Just more free.

To my dismay, that differed from how I was instructed to speak by society in general—with each growing year: less. On the porch, in the arms of my women, word choice was endless. As I grew up and away from that uncensored place, social etiquette limited the number of subjects open to discussion.

Money, politics, religion, sadness: people shifted in their seats when I asked about these things. Slowly, to avoid that uncomfortable pause where you realize you've stepped over an invisible etiquette line, I learned to stop addressing those subjects.

By the time college came, I was an expert—super polite, socially dignified. And then, at a big New England city school,

I met Joe. Perhaps the most charismatic kid from his rural town in Long Island and probably the smartest too. He never stopped talking, never stopped making everyone around him laugh and, to this day, has not stopped challenging me.

For four years, I couldn't pinpoint what exactly it was about Joe that captivated me. And then, a year into postgrad, I understood.

"*Oh my god, no no no no no.*" He sighed dramatically into the receiver of his phone. Time zones apart, forty-minute chats were our ritual. "*Kaley!*"

I giggled. "*I mean, we can totally tell each other. I just thought, you know, salary is one of those things you're not supposed to talk about.*"

"*And who made up that rule?*" He was emphatic, loud. "*The people that want to keep us underpaid and overworked, that's who! The only people that benefit from us not discussing our salaries are the people who have the power—these big corporate companies who are paying us. It's in their direct interest for us not to talk to each other because then we won't know that there are pay discrepancies. And if we don't know, then they can just keep getting away with it.*"

My phone blared as Joe continued explaining. "*Of course, it isn't always that easy,*" he admitted, with empathy. "*You could get fired for speaking out, and if you lose your job then you lose your income, and then you lose your ability to live or support a family, and you can't really afford an employment lawyer, and—*"

Moral of the story: it's scarier to be vocal when you have a lot to lose.

But as Joe plunged into a glorious retelling of the day, he announced his holiday bonus amount in the middle of his office. I considered the topics that don't make it off the porch. Between visions of sugar plums and Joe's fuming HR representative, I started thinking about the other taboo topics we're *not supposed to talk about.*

Politics, religion, sadness, sure. But also therapy. Sex. Sexual violence.

Sex is intimate: an agreement between two people, often in private. Great to talk about, fine not to. Sexual violence is intimacy's inverse. There is no agreement—there never was. Something was taken.

When something is taken by sexual violence, and we don't feel like we can discuss it, who benefits? The takers. They are free to take again and they do. An average of five more times.[11]

So, if sexual violence is one of those things you're not supposed to talk about, *who made up that rule?*

As long as the subject remains taboo, it remains unsolvable. We aren't free to talk about it openly with each other, which makes talking about it with law enforcement even less likely. Plus, the system's ineffectiveness in the area is widely known, and the negative repercussions of reporting are real. The vast majority of people do not think it's worth the potential trauma, trouble, or turmoil of reporting assault to the police. With good reason.

As long as that's all true, where can we go instead? Where we've always gone. To the front porch.

We know that front porch conversations solve problems. Those freely shared opinions, spoken with conviction in the cover of night, are vital. We also know that location is secondary. For me, it's a front porch. For you, it could be a park bench or a lengthy phone call. Revolution can begin anywhere, in the simple power of speaking vulnerably. It's born from sharing lived experiences, identifying oppressive systems, and then demanding those systems change.

---

11 David Lisak and Paul M. Miller, "Repeat Rape and Multiple Offending among Undetected Rapists," *Violence and Victims* 17, no. 1, (February 2002)

Until the system works, we must work for each other. Listen, empathize, warn. With no system to protect us, we protect each other.

In September 2018, #WhyIDidntReport trended on Twitter. It was a hashtagged reaction to the assumption that a certain Supreme Court nominee couldn't have assaulted Dr. Blasey Ford, because if he did, she would have reported.[12] No report, no assault, the forty-fifth president implied in a tweet.[13]

Not so fast, argued front porch revolutionaries everywhere, and they got digitally loud. With no system to defend them, they defended each other.

"#WhyIDidntReport
Because I was a party girl at university
Because I went home with him
Because I thought everyone would say I asked for it
Because I thought this was just what happened when you partied too hard
Because I thought no one would believe me
I thought I deserved it" [14]

"Moving forward felt more important than justice. #WhyIDidntReport" [15]

---

12   CBS News, "#WhyIDidntReport: Hundreds of Thousands Confide Their Stories of Rape, Abuse," *CBS This Morning,* September 24, 2018.

13   Donald J. Trump (@RealDonaldTrump), "I have no doubt that…," Twitter, September 21, 2018.

14   Lerato Chondoma (@blkfaerie), "#WhyIDidntReport, Because I was a party girl at university…," Twitter, September 22, 2018, 12:19 a.m.

15   Caitlyn Leong (@caitlyn_leong), "Moving forward felt more important than justice. #WhyIDidntReport," Twitter, September 22, 2018, 1:14 p.m.

"He was on the campus police force. I felt stupid because I'd trusted him. I knew no one would believe me. #WhyIDidntReport" [16]

Two hundred and eighty characters and "hundreds of thousands" of hashtags.[17] The virtual trend started very real conversations, making one thing clear: there is so much more than one reason why a person doesn't report. Way beyond 280 characters worth of reasons, in fact. There are years of reasons—from the instant we realize sex is *one of those things you're not supposed to talk about,* to the moment we watch Chanel Miller's assailant get six months in prison after a year-long trial.[18] From the morning we're told to dress more conservatively so that boys will be less creepy, to the day our country elects a president with twenty-six sexual assault allegations against him, to the somber afternoon Dr. Christine Blasey Ford's assailant takes the oath for the highest court in the land.[19]

Why don't people report?

Because why would you?

That's me, answering the question with a question, as a cis, straight, white woman. Even with a whole lot of privilege, my life experience has imparted unfortunate, but not

---

16   Dr. Julie Rohwein (@jirohweinn), "He was on the campus police force. I felt stupid because I'd trusted him. I knew no one would believe me. #WhyIDidntReport," Twitter, September 22, 2018, 1:14p.m.

17   CBS News, "#WhyIDidntReport: Hundreds of Thousands Confide Their Stories of Rape, Abuse," *CBS This Morning*, September 24, 2018.

18   Chanel Miller, *Know My Name* (New York: Viking Press, 2019), 236.

19   Eliza Relman, "The 26 Women Who Have Accused Trump of Sexual Misconduct," *Business Insider*, September 17, 2020.

unfounded, understanding: women's stories don't matter. Not enough to create change.

And that's coming from someone who identifies as an optimist! I want to believe in inherent goodness, to believe that society and the systems we've built work. Yet, when I look inward and hear shadowy memories of *That's too much cleavage* and *Well, what do you think gave him that impression?* the best I can come up with is still just, *Why would you?*

Then I look outward. And that *Why would you?* becomes even more obvious. Amidst a swarm of documented cases in which authorities are racist, homophobic, or ineffective, at best, and fatally violent, at worst, it seems silly to even ask, *Why don't people report?*

When I sat down to write this book, I was looking for a list of reasons. There were lists online, full academic studies on why people don't report sexual violence, but they all seemed to be missing something.

Instead, I focused on the tangible: the women who were willing to respond, to engage, to have front-porch conversations with me. They each spoke candidly about the overlapping, sometimes indescribable reasons they didn't report. The details of their stories spun in my head for months, and in studying their similarities, a list started to emerge on its own.

To validate my intuition, I got in touch with a professional: Detective Carrie Hull.

A former police officer, she is a reassurance that, even within a system that is racist and sexist, there are people attempting to operate with integrity and compassion. When I got her on the phone, I launched into the list of reasons I'd come up with. She listened, patiently, before saying:

"You know, in all my years of doing this, the one thing I keep coming back to is that you cannot come up with a predefined list to solve this problem. And, by trying to do that, I think we really create more silence around it. By giving people ways to fit into a solution, instead of allowing them to opt into their own solution, we make people uncomfortable."

Turns out, the only piece missing was that knowledge. The women were the list I was looking for. And it was their differences, as much as their similarities, that mattered.

You'll notice the way their stories intersect, converge, and dance with each other, not around each other. While each woman cites a different main reason for not reporting, none of them had just one. Unreporting isn't neat.

We aren't supposed to talk about sexual violence. People shift in their seats; the topic makes them uncomfortable. It's an off-limits topic, and so, even though our mothers and grandmothers have lived it before us, there are so few road maps for how to heal. In staying silent about what happened and how we managed to pull through after, we are also silent about the small victories. The moments of happiness, clarity, meaning. We're alone in them.

Here, women share who they are beyond sexual assault and violence. Who they were before, after, and as a result thereof. They speak frankly about why reporting wasn't an option and under what circumstances it might have been.

This book is the front porch. Filled with genuine, brazen souls. What you'll find here is the same as what you'd find on any front porch like mine: honest, free, revolutionary stories.

ALL THAT YOU WON'T

———

"Mutato nomine de te fabula narratur"—or,
"Change only the name and this story is also about you."

—HORACE

You're on the front porch with us now. Carried here with the salt air; surrounded by feminine stories like fingers in your hair.

The honest way women share their life experiences with one another has always been sacred. To hold space for it here without breaking that vital girl-to-girl trust, I concealed all recognizable details of the unreported stories shared. Working together with the storytellers themselves, I changed names and locations, and occasionally pieces of many women's experiences have been attributed to one. Through ongoing dialog and written permission, I sought to protect the anonymity these women were afforded by not reporting. While the specifics of their stories are intentionally vague, the essence remains clear. In a law enforcement system that wasn't built for women, we don't report. We simply report back to each other.

We.

Another intentionally vague word. Here, I use it as a stand-in for the term "victims" or "survivors"—half because I don't know which is more fitting, and half because I can't use either word when telling my own story without my voice wavering a bit.

As with so many aspects of this subject matter, there's no consensus on whether "victim" or "survivor" is the word-choice *du jour* for those who have experienced sexual violence. The media seems to have settled on "survivor," but bloggers push back. The Rape, Abuse & Incest National Network (RAINN) uses both terms and urges others to simply ask the person they're referring to which they prefer.[20] When deciding which term to reference over and over and over while writing this book, though, that was not definite enough. Contradictory, indecisive research was getting me nowhere.

Technicalities weren't much help either. The word "victim" comes from the Latin root "vict," which means, "to conquer." Its sister, "victor," is "the conqueror," leaving "victim" as its inverse.[21] "The conquered?" That didn't feel right. But then neither did "survivor," which is a fusion of the Latin prefix "super," which means "over, beyond," and the verb, "vivere"— to live.[22] Technically speaking, a survivor is a person who has lived beyond or overcome. Depending on the situation, though, that may not fit. When speaking broadly about people who did or didn't report sexual violence? It doesn't.

---

20   "Key Terms and Phrases," RAINN (Rape, Abuse & Incest National Network), accessed February 19, 2021.

21   "Victim or Victor?" *Random Lightbulb Moments*, January 23, 2012.

22   Online Etymology Dictionary, s.v. "Survive (v.)," accessed February 19, 2021.

In an effort to consult another part of my brain, I subverted research and technicalities in favor of feelings. "Victim" is so often associated with pity that it's almost synonymous with feeling small. Warranted or not (and in the case of sexual violence, it's not), the word echoes with implications of weakness, fragility, helplessness. "Victim" is never something a person decides to be. Another person decides it for them, in a moment beyond their control, and then leaves the newly-branded victim to piece that term into their identity. Victims don't have a choice.

And then there's "survivor." This word is empowering to many, rightfully so. Media outlets stamp stories with this term, creating headlines that feel inherently positive. RAINN likes to reserve it for those who have "gone through the recovery process," which makes sense, according to its etymology.[23] While "victim" feels small, "survivor" conjures connotations of strength. The word feels massive and commemorative and complete. The problem? There is nothing to achieve, no celebratory final step, when "going through the recovery process" after sexual violence.

While identifying as a victim made me cringe beneath the weight of my own story, trying to live up to the term "survivor" made me confused. From a feelings standpoint, neither did the trick.

Left without a word to describe those who have experienced sexual violence, I decided to call them "people." Revelatory, for sure. But considering how many of us live through this trauma, either as the primary subject or an adjacent secondary character, it seems like the only accurate designation.

---

23 "Key Terms and Phrases," RAINN (Rape, Abuse & Incest National Network), accessed February 19, 2021.

After tallying up those who experience sexual violence, their friends and family, plus the assailants and their respective circles, you've pretty much accounted for everyone. All people.

A more specific moniker is theirs to choose.

The only person who deserves to have a name assigned to them without being asked is the perpetrator. The assailant. They took control from another person, and in that moment, they chose to categorize themselves as a: perp, assailant, harasser, rapist. There's no room for debate in calling them what they are. In anonymous retellings, no time was spent making up names for assailants. In case studies pulled from the media, their names are not reprinted. They don't deserve the notoriety, the humanization. In this book, they exist simply in relation to the person they harmed.

Here, we are interested in that whole, complex, resilient person.

For the same reason, you won't find graphic or explicit details of assault here. The focus is on the person's empowered decision not to report, and on their ever-evolving healing process after that decision. Not on the minutes where an assailant took a vastly different decision from them. When interviewing our storytellers, I didn't ask about the nitty-gritty of those moments. When it comes to the sacred process of sharing stories, it doesn't matter where someone was violated, or exactly how.

As a society, we get caught up in the whos and whens and hows of sexual violence. Naturally, we're drawn to the most obscene aspects of any evil act. Maybe it's an effort to understand and protect ourselves. If we know exactly what happened, we can ensure the same doesn't happen to us. Right? Cancel culture leads us to bury individual perps, which is essential, but we don't pause to evaluate which systems should be cancelled as well. We see a person through her brave report, follow her while media coverage lasts, but don't check in on how her life continues to unfold thereafter. In the details, the story gets lost.

And it's there—between beginning, middle, and end—where understanding occurs. Through the nuances of story, we can understand the flaws in our system. When we sit and feel why a person wouldn't report, we are better equipped to rebuild a system in which they would.

LAKES

"We fight to say you can't. We fight for accountability. We fight to establish precedent. We fight because we pray we'll be the last ones to feel this kind of pain."

—CHANEL MILLER

Like any porch worth visiting, there are a couple of women already here. I like to imagine them glorious, content, basking. A screened-in porch, after all, lets in fresh air and sunlight. And it keeps out unwanted pests.

Which is to say, I like to imagine them reveling in so much more than what they got.

Chanel Miller and Dr. Christine Blasey Ford: their respective cases are two of the most impactful incidents of reported sexual violence in the past decade. One changed laws, and the other was broadcast on TVs across the country. They have both carried sheer cultural magnitude since their coverage began. It's easy to imagine that when a person is deciding whether or not to report, they might look to these cases for reference. So, as we listen to unreports and understand the flaws of the system, it's crucial to recognize the context that Chanel and Christine's coverage created.

While my personal story unfolds by the ocean, theirs are like lakes. In this book, everything flows into them.

CHRISTINE

Before the nation knew her, Dr. Christine Blasey Ford was regarded. At the risk of sounding unclear, let me explain.

Christine Blasey Ford, with her honey-blonde hair and precise, measured tone, is not just known but respected in many circles. She works in the psychiatry department at Stanford School of Medicine, is widely published within her field, and taught at Palo Alto University for seven years. Propelled by her dutiful spirit, she went to undergrad at University of North Carolina at Chapel Hill, and then earned three advanced degrees from Pepperdine, Stanford, and the University of Southern California. Highly regarded education; highly regarded professional.[24]

Autumn 2018 stands in sharp contrast to the rest of her life. That October she was disregarded. But it hadn't been the first time.

Even before her degrees and career accolades and earning the "Dr." prefix, high-school Christine—or "Chrissy" as friends called her—was an all-star. A three-sport athlete, she was popular and well liked. "She was the sort of person a lot of people paid attention to. She was a leader; she was great," remembered a male friend.[25]

And then things changed: she went to a party. As a teenager, that's often where things change. Soaked in the promise

---

24 Elizabeth Williamson, Rebecca R. Ruiz, Emily Steel, Grace Ashford and Steve Eder, "For Christine Blasey Ford, a Drastic Turn from a Quiet Life in Academia," *New York Times*, September 19, 2018.

25 Ibid.

of summer and beer and a lack of adults, parties can accelerate friendships and relationships and abbreviate the long path to adulthood, even just for a night. So, with her swimsuit still on after a day at the pool and half her high school career behind her, she did the normal, summery, teenage thing to do: went to a house where, more likely than not, parents were away for the night.[26]

At that party, she had to go to the bathroom—also very typical, as anyone who's been to a party can attest to. But while she blazed her way upstairs, convention faded.

Chrissy was pushed into a bedroom by a fellow partygoer and his "very drunken" friend. She described what happened next in a letter to Senator Dianne Feinstein thirty-six summers later: [27]

The boys "locked the door and played loud music ... [Her young assailant] then pushed her on a bed, began grinding his body against hers and tried to undress her ... To stifle her screams ... he covered her mouth with his hand," the letter alleges.

The drunk sidekick "told his friend to alternately 'go for it' and 'stop,'" until he finally "jumped on the bed, causing the three teenagers to tumble onto the floor."

At this point, she ran from the room, locked herself in the bathroom and escaped after hearing the two inebriated boys stumbling down the stairs.[28]

---

26 The New York Times, "Read Christine Blasey Ford's Prepared Statement," *New York Times*, September 26, 2018.

27 Elizabeth Williamson, Rebecca R. Ruiz, Emily Steel, Grace Ashford and Steve Eder, "For Christine Blasey Ford, a Drastic Turn from a Quiet Life in Academia," *New York Times*, September 19, 2018.

28 "Read the Letter Christine Blasey Ford Sent Accusing Brett Kavanaugh of Sexual Misconduct," *CNN*, September 17, 2018.

By the time Chrissy made it to the bathroom, everything had changed. During the forced detour, she had been disregarded in the most awful way: the boy assailant disregarded her consent. And that type of disregard leaves a mark.

In the months and years that followed, she "fell off the face of the earth socially," according to a friend. "All I remember is after my junior year thinking, 'Where's Chrissy Blasey?'"[29]

She stopped showing up at events where she was once a staple. No more normal, teenage parties for her. She graduated high school, spent years in higher education, and along the way, "Chrissy" disappeared—replaced by "Dr." and "Christine." She married in 2002, adding another name: "Ford." Together with her husband, she bought two houses in California. On one, she insisted they install a second front door.[30]

"Our house does not look aesthetically pleasing from the curb," she concedes.[31] That seems fitting: the reason for that second front door is not appealing either.

Until 2012, Christine did not talk in detail to anyone about the summer party that left its mark on her world. When the story came out for the first time, it was on a couch, next to a baffled husband. They were in couples therapy, debating the need for their second front door.[32]

---

29 Elizabeth Williamson, Rebecca R. Ruiz, Emily Steel, Grace Ashford and Steve Eder, "For Christine Blasey Ford, a Drastic Turn from a Quiet Life in Academia," *New York Times*, September 19, 2018.

30 The New York Times, "Read Christine Blasey Ford's Prepared Statement," *New York Times,* September 26, 2018.

31 "Kavanaugh hearing: Transcript," September 27, 2018, The Washington Post, transcript.

32 Elizabeth Williamson, Rebecca R. Ruiz, Emily Steel, Grace Ashford and Steve Eder, "For Christine Blasey Ford, a Drastic Turn from a Quiet Life in Academia," *New York Times*, September 19, 2018.

Christine explained to her husband why she was so adamant about having another escape route; after that, the door stayed. And that was it. For the next eight years, Christine turned her focus forward once more and continued to become regarded within her field. She developed a test to assess how young children cope with trauma and wrote a widely-used statistics guide.[33] At night, she came home to two adoring sons, two front doors, and a husband who understood.

One night, she came home to more. News: the forty-fifth president of the United States had named his pick for the newest Supreme Court justice. Christine knew the name. Despite the thirty-six years she'd spent trying to forget it, she knew.

After fierce internal debate, she penned the letter to Senator Dianne Feinstein in late-summer 2018. In the note, she objected to this man, her boy assailant, having a spot on the highest court in the land. He'd been chosen to uphold justice from a position of prestige—a position from which the American people would depend on him to be good, honest, fair. In Christine's memory, he did not exist as any of those things. Doing her civic duty, she alerted the system with the power to stop him.

That system did not thank Christine. It did not commend her for doing the right thing and then follow her brave lead, condemning her assailant. It did not consider another name on the lengthy list of qualified candidates. Instead, the system yanked Christine from her life in academia, thrust her into the center of a courtroom, and made her testify before the entire country. She devoted months of her life, sacrificed her private citizenship, and hired a team of (female) lawyers.

---

33 Ibid.

Despite her legal team's ask, there was no FBI investigation before her testimony.[34]

In the weeks leading up to her appearance in court, she became a topic of conversation nationwide. Social media lit her name up in its overwhelming fluorescent hue. But the tags and hashtags did not make her a household name in an entirely positive way.

"I have been called the most vile and hateful names imaginable," she said in her Senate testimony. "People have posted my personal information on the internet. This has resulted in additional emails, calls, and threats. My family and I were forced to move out of our home."[35]

Even those who were posting about her supportively, using words like "heroic" to describe her, acknowledged that any praise she may have received hardly outweighed the pain.

"Seeing what people say, I really, really understand why somebody wouldn't want to be a part of this discussion," said Christine's best friend from college, Catherine Piwowarski. "I think it is brave. But it is a lot to take on."[36]

Christine came to the hearing with polygraph results, notes from her therapist, and a years-long list of measurable effects the assault had on her. She could detail the mark it left. And yet, she was lambasted for not remembering minor details of the moments on her way to the bathroom. The President mocked her openly at a rally, and members of the

34 Ibid.

35 "Kavanaugh hearing: Transcript," September 27, 2018, The Washington Post, transcript.

36 Elizabeth Williamson, Rebecca R. Ruiz, Emily Steel, Grace Ashford and Steve Eder, "For Christine Blasey Ford, a Drastic Turn from a Quiet Life in Academia," New York Times, September 19, 2018.

senate discredited her narrative due to lack of specifics.[37] When you Google her name, to this day, the page one search results look something like this:

Sen. Ron Johnson Suggests Christine Blasey Ford May Have 'False Memories'...[38]

21 Reasons Not to Believe Ford's Claims About Justice Kavanaugh[39]

Christine Blasey Ford's Lies and Other Commentary[40]

Months before the hearing, according to an account in *The San Jose Mercury News*, Christine told a friend, "I've been trying to forget this all my life, and now I'm supposed to remember every little detail." What a raw, torturous way to face your most painful memory: under the scrutiny of an entire country.[41]

The boy assailant's friend, who grew up to author a book about blacking out as a teenager, testified that he did not remember his friend committing the assault. This is the accomplice Christine remembers as being "very drunken." It cannot be overstated: he grew up to write a book on blacking out. And yet, his denial held weight.

37 Jordyn Phelps, "Trump Mocks Christine Blasey Ford, Who Accused Kavanaugh of Sexual Assault," *ABC News*, October 3, 2018.

38 Daniel Bice, "Bice: Sen. Ron Johnson Suggests Christine Blasey Ford May Have 'False Memories' of Alleged Assault," *Milwaukee Journal Sentinel*, September 29, 2018.

39 Mollie Hemingway and Carrie Severino, "21 Reasons Not to Believe Christine Blasey Ford's Claims about Justice Kavanaugh," *The Federalist*, December 2, 2019.

40 Post Editorial Board, "Christine Blasey Ford's Lies and Other Commentary," *New York Post*, December 2, 2019.

41 Elizabeth Williamson, Rebecca R. Ruiz, Emily Steel, Grace Ashford and Steve Eder, "For Christine Blasey Ford, a Drastic Turn from a Quiet Life in Academia," *New York Times*, September 19, 2018.

Before going public with her allegations, Christine said she asked herself, "Why suffer through the annihilation if it's not going to matter?"[42]

The boy assailant now sits on the Supreme Court.

Despite reassuring articles about how she "did not come forward in vain," and as necessary as it is to account for the way her courage inspired many, her testimony did not stop the assailant from his appointment. Hers is not a story people look to and see justice in. It was a negative, intimidating, life-altering experience—and as long as her boy assailant rules from a position of extreme power, no logical observer can conclude that, yes, it was worth it for Christine to suffer the annihilation.

So why don't people report?

When discussing whether Christine's testimony mattered to him, the senator who scheduled the vote to advance her assailant said: "I found Dr. Ford's testimony credible. There is simply no reason to deny [the alleged boy assailant] a place on the Supreme Court." [43]

In other words, he believed her. He just didn't think it mattered.

If the front porch taught me anything at a very young age, it was that we become walking, breathing accumulations of our stories. Books in our own right—pieced together by chapters that make us simultaneously more similar and more different. Our stories are our essence. To disregard a person's story is to disregard her being.

---

42 Emma Brown, "California Professor, Writer of Confidential Brett Kavanaugh Letter, Speaks Out about Her Allegation of Sexual Assault," *The Washington Post,* September 16, 2018.

43 John Cassidy, "The Senate Republican's Less-Than-Human Treatment of Christine Blasey Ford," *The New Yorker,* September 28, 2018.

Christine's story was disregarded. A majority vote took place, expressing indifference for her humanity.

In our society, with our current systems, no number of degrees can save you. No matter how highly regarded you become as a professor, a researcher, an author, you can and will still be disregarded when reporting sexual violence. Instead of admitting sexism or owning their decision to disregard her, the senators who approved her boy assailant blamed it on Christine's lack of report.

No report, no justice, they seemed to say. Implying that if there had been a report after that party in the summer of 1982, there would have been justice.

But let's examine a story that could back that up—the second of the widely-covered sexual assault cases this book pours into. Chanel Miller reported right away. Did she get justice?

CHANEL

The only thing more captivating than Chanel Miller's elegant aptitude is her graceful vulnerability. Her book, *Know My Name*, is candid and fair in its evaluation of just about everything—but especially in its evaluation of our country's criminal justice system.

Chanel did not get to choose whether to report. She was found by police officers behind a dumpster. Photographed, clothes askew, she was unconsciously hoisted up out of the crime scene and into the hospital, where the rape response team took over. She never had the chance to decide if authorities should know her story because, as first responders, they already did. But then her younger sister picked her up at the hospital. And during that car ride, wrapped in a new sweatshirt from the response team and a vague sense of confusion, Chanel began the process of deciding who else she'd report to. She revealed her assault to her family and friends one by one, and then eventually to the entire world.[44]

Her assault. Isn't it wild that, when a perpetrator takes advantage of you, the assault becomes yours?

I remember wishing so deeply to give it back, in the days and weeks after mine was handed to me. *I didn't ask for this—can't I put it back where it came from? Can't it be his to deal with?* I wondered if Chanel felt the same way. Wrapped in my own vague sense of confusion, one thing was clear. We were all more alike than I'd realized.

But it is important to note where Chanel differs from many of the people in this book: she had the report. The official, on-record evaluation by police officers and a hospital. The report that, by senatorial implication, might have granted her justice.

Did it? Well, that depends how you define justice.

Chanel was found—rescued?—in 2015. Two Swedish bikers saw a man on top of her limp body behind a dumpster and called the police. The bikers confronted the man, who it turns out, was really just a boy. A freshman swimmer from a nearby university. As they began questioning him, he ran.[45] Maybe it's just my non-athletic disposition, but I've always believed that when people run, it's a sign: something terrible is happening.

Chanel woke up into a new identity: "Emily Doe."[46] Used in court documents and coverage, the alias shielded her from notoriety within her own life—her coworkers, friends, and even family wouldn't know she was the woman who had been

---

44 Chanel Miller, *Know My Name* (New York: Viking Press, 2019), 4, 19, 37.

45 Ibid.

46 Ibid.

assaulted by the freshman boy unless she told them. But there were other, more unavoidable repercussions of reporting that "Emily" didn't shield her from. Though her name wasn't used, Chanel was still haunted by the media coverage and online commentary on her case.

In America, the media has evolved into a system that works in tandem with the justice system when it comes to sexual violence. Many people report there, instead of to the police. In a lot of ways, it has historically been just as flawed. In this case, it was.

Articles on the incident ended with her freshman assailant's swim times, as if complimenting him on his accomplishments after naming him as the perpetrator. The comments beneath those articles read degrading, victim-blaming sentiments: "What was she doing at a frat party?"; "This isn't really rape"; "Why was she alone?"; "She's the predator 'cause she's older"; "Why would you ever get that drunk?"[47] Chanel scrolled through them, surfing a virtual world that was strikingly different than the reality she was living. "It was endless," she recalled in a *60 Minutes* interview.[48]

In 1992, Helen Benedict published a book called *Virgin or Vamp: How the Press Covers Sex Crimes*. She spends 309 pages urging journalists to be conscientious in their coverage of sexual violence: to avoid alluding to the "virgin" or "vamp" trope. Generally, best to avoid all tropes, she concludes.

Decades later, the resurgent #MeToo movement reinvigorated the emphasis on fair, non-glamorized media

47 Katie J.M. Baker, "Here's the Powerful Letter the Stanford Victim Read to Her Attacker," *Buzzfeed*, June 3, 2016.

48 60 Minutes, "Chanel Miller," reporting by Bill Whitaker, September 22, 2019, video.

treatment for sex crimes. If Chanel's story made headlines in 2017, instead of 2015, I wonder if the articles would have been written differently. Maybe, at the very least, they wouldn't have included the freshman assailant's swim times.

But in 2015, as Chanel put it: "[The press was] framing it like he had so much to lose and were not focusing on what had already been lost, for me."[49]

In the throes of her reported assault, and the criminal case that came with it, what exactly was lost?

"Your damage was concrete; stripped of titles, degrees, enrollment. My damage was internal, unseen," she wrote in her viral victim statement, which addresses the freshman assailant directly. "I carry it with me. You took away my worth, my privacy, my energy, my time, my safety, my intimacy, my confidence, my own voice … ."[50]

The entire process, from violation to conviction, took a year and a half. For eighteen months in her early-to-mid-twenties, Chanel (under her "Emily" pseudonym) fought a battle she did not choose. A battle she was dragged into. "At the of end of the hearing … I was too tired to speak. I would leave drained, silent. I would go home, turn off my phone, and for days I would not speak," Chanel continued, in her victim statement.[51]

In the *60 Minutes* segment on Chanel, her defense attorney Alaleh Kianerci explained that the mere concept of going to court is traumatic to begin with. "It is incredibly difficult for a victim of sexual assault to walk into court in front of

---

49 Ibid.

50 Katie J.M. Baker, "Here's the Powerful Letter the Stanford Victim Read to Her Attacker," *Buzzfeed,* June 3, 2016.

51 Ibid.

their perpetrator and recount the worst thing that happened to them in a room full of strangers," she said. [52]

Stretch that process over the course of eighteen months, and it's almost unbearable. Chanel remarked that, during those months spent meeting with lawyers and trekking to and from the court room, she "felt like [she] was assaulted multiple times."[53] Recounting the worst thing that happened to her was hard enough. The other side's attempt to acquit the freshman assailant of his crime made it devastating.

"I was told that because I couldn't remember, I technically could not prove it was unwanted. And that distorted me, damaged me, almost broke me," she began. "It is the saddest type of confusion to be told I was assaulted ... blatantly out in the open, but we don't know if it counts as assault yet. I had to fight for an entire year to make it clear that there was something wrong with this situation."[54]

What is there to make clear, when Chanel was unconscious and her freshman assailant ran from the scene? The Swedes who found her knew there was something wrong within seconds. Why did it take the criminal justice system more than a year to grasp the same?

"It is enough to be suffering," she added. "It is another thing to have someone ruthlessly working to diminish the gravity of validity of this suffering."[55]

---

52 60 Minutes, "Chanel Miller," reporting by Bill Whitaker, September 22, 2019, video.

53 Ibid.

54 Katie J.M. Baker, "Here's the Powerful Letter the Stanford Victim Read to Her Attacker," *Buzzfeed*, June 3, 2016.

55 Ibid.

Chanel openly admits that healing was crucial, and it was a priority for her in the days, months, and years post assault. But the criminal justice system and the media coverage made that recovery difficult, if not impossible. She so deeply needed to recover, but because headlines and hearings impeded that ability, Chanel suffered more than she would have.

"Instead of taking time to heal, I was taking time to recall the night in excruciating detail, in order to prepare for the attorney's questions that would be invasive, aggressive, and designed to steer me off course, to contradict myself," she said.[56]

Eventually, it came time for Chanel to step out of the system—time for the court case to conclude, time for a verdict. And perhaps it was in her relief, after eighteen long months, that she found compassion.

"I told the probation officer I do not want [the freshman assailant] to rot away in prison. I did not say he does not deserve to be behind bars," she remembered. "I also told the probation officer that what I truly wanted was for [the freshman assailant] to get it, to understand and admit to his wrongdoing."[57]

The only problem with an admission of wrongdoing? The gravity of a sincere, "I'm sorry" is unaccounted for in our current system. Currently, there is not only a lack of space for healing; there's a lack of space for apology as well. As with many aspects of our increasingly polarized society, in court there are two options: acquittal or conviction. "I'm sorry" lives somewhere between the two. To apologize is to confirm two truths: *"Yes, I did it, and yes, I wish with every fiber of my*

---

56 Ibid.

57 Ibid.

being that I didn't do it." No matter how important it is for the person who has been hurt to hear the second truth —the *"I wish I didn't"*—a defendant simply can't risk muttering the first. They can't even imply: *"Yes, I did it."*

Not when news cameras everywhere are waiting to blast that soundbite, and viral clickbait headlines will summarize their statement crudely. Not when acquittal and conviction are the only two options. For a defendant, fear of their own impending doom is heavier than the feelings of the person they hurt. To say "I'm sorry" is to seal themselves into a conviction. So, even if they sense the other person needs to hear an apology, they don't dare deliver one.

Without space for apology, the defendant does not have much of a choice beyond fierce and offensive denial. And the options of the hurt person become limited too. It's basic balance-maintaining rules: when one steps out of the gray area into blackness, the other must step into the white. In the elusive space of sexual violence, doesn't it make sense to consider the gray? To make space for "I'm sorry?"

didn't get an apology. She got a freshman assailant who crafted a rigid and harsh defense, and she became their counterbalance. For eighteen months, she was "the accuser" to his "the accused."

Chanel had thorns in her hair. She had cuts and bruises. She had the official report, the rape kit; evidence that doesn't exist, in many cases of sexual violence. And then, after spending a large part of her twenties as "the accuser," her assailant finally got his sentence.

Six months in prison.

Chanel was confined to her trial for a year and a half. She was jailed by her alias, "Emily Doe." When it came time for a verdict, the freshman rapist got a third of that time in prison.[58] So if the assumption is that a report unequivocally translates to justice, I guess it depends how you define the latter. I would not define it as a six-month term.

---

58 Ibid.

PRIVATE LIFE

———

"Apart from the assault itself, these last couple of
weeks have been the hardest of my life. I have had
to relive my trauma in front of the entire world."
—DR. CHRISTINE BLASEY FORD

Sometimes a circumstance is just plain acidic. You know the moment you taste it, when the tang bounces around your mouth and your nose crinkles in aversion and you wish you were anywhere but right there, digesting the unpleasantness that just happened.

Those who have tasted their own bile in such a situation know there's a litmus test you can use to see if others agree. It's a simple experiment, a quick hypothesis and conclusion, and it exists entirely in people's eyes right after you tell them. Was that thing you lived through actually acidic? Mention it to someone, and you'll find out. It will be reflected back in the way they look at you—just look at you—for a second. A low pH is evident in the silence that lasts a moment too long, in the way the corners of a person's eyes fall while their eyebrows raise. They aren't asking you if you're okay (they know that acid burns). It's more like they're asking themselves how you'll ever be okay.

One of my new friends, Elle, confirmed acidity for me the morning after, in a whisper through the phone. *"Yes, that's rape,"* she said. And that unspoken question hung between us.

My oldest friend, MK, took the litmus test days later. She stopped our lifelong, always-chattering conversation and just looked at me for a minute. The silence confirmed it, and we both wondered:

What should I do next, to be okay?

Right after any just-plain-acidic thing, that answer isn't anywhere. When I look back at photos of myself from the days, the weeks, the summer after, I can see its absence in my eyes. There's uncertainty in the way they never crease completely with my smile. They're always a little too watery with tears I refused to cry. Cloudy and confused, what ripples across them is clear: the undeniable, unreported, acidic new life experience.

We'll get into that story later.

ISLA

Back to Isla. Isla and her thickly-freckled cheeks and toothy smile. Isla and her easy blonde hair, white Superga sneakers, and wide, brown eyes. Remember Isla? She was spending the summer exploring the space between freshman and sophomore at Santa Monica High. The oldest of five, with protective parents who worked in television. The happy, trusting teen who was banned from parties after midnight, getting into cars with people she didn't know, and smoking weed. The beach-city kid who was practically sheltered, when compared to her peers.

Isla: the fourteen-year-old with a priority to become less so.

She lit up the party that night—standard. She always glowed with that casual confidence that East Coasters recognize as totally Californian. But the turn of the school year had been especially kind to her, instilling a new sense of *knowing* that can only be achieved after freshman year.

She lit it up until 11:59 p.m., when her parents rolled into the driveway and called her. After three redials, she picked up, said her goodbyes, and walked out—also standard. She sat quietly, maybe mopey, in the back seat during their Hollywood Hills drive home, and flicked open Facebook on her iPhone 4. With the exchange of a few messages, that night was set up to become the least standard of her entire life.

He lived down the street, was a couple years older, and had been Facebook-flirting with her for a few weeks. He had a car and, if there was any way she could sneak out, of course he could come scoop her up. She found a way.

Summer's hot promise of possibility makes us all a little more teenager. It's the season of flings and freedom and foolishness. Grown men play like seven-year-olds, and seven-year-olds bike a street ahead of their parents. Shoes become a second thought as weekends go from being enjoyed to being lived. If summer were a high schooler, it would be a sophomore: knowing and daring, but still young and frivolous enough. Its effect on actual high school sophomores, then, is by default exponential.

That night, Isla was a summery teen to the nth degree: a nonfreshman with a crush and an opportunity. Wind at her back, she slipped out of her bedroom and raced to the car, beaming. He didn't mention that his friend would be along for the ride, but when she climbed into the car and realized, it didn't shake her. Adrenaline pumping, she was once again in the hills, but this ride could not be more different than the one she'd taken an hour before. The mysterious friend in the back seat offered up his house as a destination, and they flew toward it. Isla stuck her hand out the window, fingers spread, and let the dark heat blow in, out, around. The radio vibrated through speakers, the boys laughed, and Isla felt whatever the exact opposite of sheltered is.

When Isla and the boys landed at the house, a second wave of adrenaline hit. She knew this house. Everyone knew this house. It belonged to the famous actor who moved into her neighborhood a few years back, which meant a couple of things. First, they weren't as far from her parents as their Californian cruise had made it seem. Second, she realized, glancing behind her with a new sense of wonder, back-seat boy was the famous actor's son.

That nonstandard night was one of Isla's first experiences drinking, even if it was just a couple of beers. It was her first time trying weed, even if it was just a puff. And, perhaps consequentially, it was her first time blacking out. Hours later, it was her first time waking up completely naked, bleeding, with back-seat boy's body on top of her. Her first time trying to wake the pair of sleeping boys, and when they wouldn't listen to her, her first time walking home in the dark at night.

That's how sunny, fourteen-year-old Isla experienced sex for the first time. That's also how she gained a couple of new, very different, priorities: protect herself, protect her family, and heal.

"I was just a wannabe devious child," she says now, in hindsight. "So, when that happened, I thought, *Well, I was told not to do these things, so no one's gonna feel bad for me. No one's gonna sympathize with me, because I got myself into this situation.* I didn't tell my parents because I snuck out of the house, and I was more worried about the repercussions of that than I was about the reality of what happened to me."

When she did tell someone—a friend—they responded bluntly: *"You just don't remember, but you probably wanted it to happen. You were gonna lose your virginity anyways, so be thankful. Now it's over with. Now you don't have to worry about it."*

For years after, she didn't tell anyone else.

Instead, she focused on recreating a sense of safety around her. She transferred out of Santa Monica High School into a new school in the district and never messaged the older boy or his friend again.

Two years later, Obama was reelected, Miley and Liam got engaged, and "Call Me Maybe" took over as the song of the summer. Isla decided to share the story with her parents, who confirmed: it was an acidic circumstance. Then she left for college on the East Coast where, surrounded by a group of girls, her healing process continued. She began to share her story, and for some friends she became a guide during the aftermath of assault when it happened to them.

But she's cautious. "Even thinking about it to this day," she states frankly, "it scares me to think that people who know him might find out that I had this experience with him and choose not to believe me."

Isla was aware of the fact that plenty of people knew back-seat boy—or at least, they knew his big-screen dad. She remembers thinking to herself that the story would definitely get media attention if she reported and it got into the wrong hands. They were neighbors. Close enough to walk, bleeding, from one house to another in the middle of the night. If this got out, even just on a small scale, would her family have to move? As the oldest of five children, Isla imagined how the almost certain exposure would affect her siblings.

The way Isla strings words together is still that unique combination of relaxed and intelligent that feels exclusive to the West Coast. But there's something more, something beneath.

"I remember I didn't want them to see me that way," she says, voice snagging a bit. "As a victim of something." She didn't want to watch them take the litmus test. To see the corners of their eyes fall while their eyebrows raised. To feel them wonder about the question she didn't know the answer to yet: *What should she do next, to be okay?*

So, she didn't report. She avoided losing control over the way her siblings saw her and the way the community saw their family. She saved them all from mass media exposure. Plus, she says, she doubts the reporting process would've helped her much anyway.

"Maybe going to the authorities would have liberated me a little bit, but it really would depend on the outcome of what happened. All I could do would be to tell my truth, and tell my story," she hesitates. "But if no one did anything to help me get the justice that I felt I deserved, I would have just made myself vulnerable and exposed my deepest wound to people just for them to, you know, throw salt on it."

Instead, she focused on healing that wound.

Ten years later, as a new decade begins around her, Isla is back in Los Angeles and taking fierce notice of the world around her. She writes poetry, practices photography, and, with the help of a therapist, has redefined intimacy for herself. She continues to be a positive resource to several of her friends as they struggle with sexual assault issues of their own, and, finally, has settled into a healthy relationship.

She's the first to admit she still wrestles with memories of that summer night before her sophomore year, the night she developed a new set of priorities: protect herself, protect her family, and heal. But she is happy, grounded, and incredibly self-aware. When asked how she tackled her third priority—healing—she has a simple answer.

"With time."

LAUREN

The press can't report on a crime that's unreported. Even a salacious, celebrity-kid scandal, a would-be clickbait phenomenon; the media can't grab hold of that story if it doesn't exist. Isla made sure of that.

Lauren O'Connor was assaulted at age twenty-three, but that's not why her name ended up in the *New York Times*. She told her roommate about the assault the next day but decided not to report to any type of system. She made the same choice Isla did; the press couldn't grab hold of her story. Today, that assault is an underreported aspect of her narrative—perhaps by design.[59]

Lauren values her privacy. But despite that value, and despite her early-twenties' unreport, her name was still printed all over media outlets. Without her control or intent, "Lauren O'Connor" returns more than just a few Google results.

The line between public figure and private citizen can be an elusive one. So often in cases of sexual assault and rape, both the assailant and their target are plastered all over the press, thrust into public figure territory. Even if only for a short period of time, the effects of that coverage can continue detonating for years.

But, again, Lauren didn't report when she was assaulted.

Even though she wasn't always going to be a public figure, Lauren was always going to be successful. With dark-auburn

---

59 Mike Bayer, "Lauren O'Connor on 'The Coach Mike Podcast'," *Los Angeles Times*, March 20, 2020, video, 2:23.

hair, sharp features, and undeniable ambition, Lauren conquered the University of Virginia's undergraduate program.
She ran more or less every club related to both her majors
before graduating in 2009 with four short films under her belt.[60]

Cue her entrance to the world of film and television. In
that world, known for making public figures, Lauren found
her niche way behind the camera, in development. A private
position for a private person.

She was that infectious combination of driven and personable—the type who works hard and rises quickly. She landed
at The Weinstein Company at the height of her mid-twenties,
as an exceptionally young development executive.[61]

It sounds like I'm listing a resume, and that's because I
am. Lauren's work is integral to every part of her story.

Lauren was excelling, and the opportunities the position
provided her were unmatched. She took the job, stayed at the
job, and stayed silent on the job for as long as she could. Then
one night, a young woman came to her sobbing, inconsolably
attempting to detail the situation she'd just escaped: the way
a powerful producer, who may or may not have also been the
company's namesake, violated her.[62]

Lauren's silence stopped. She drafted a clear, in-depth
memo detailing the mistreatment of women she had seen
and experienced at The Weinstein Company.[63] Driven by
her fury for that tearful woman in a way she hadn't been

60 Lauren O'Connor's LinkedIn profile, accessed February 19, 2021.

61 Ibid.

62 Lauren O'Connor, interview by Amy Goodman, *Democracy Now!*
    January 29, 2019.

63 Jodi Kantor and Megan Twohey, *She Said* (New York: Penguin Press,
    2019), 135.

driven by fury for herself years earlier, she reported. But she did not abandon caution.

Subject: "For your records"

Message: "As requested, I took some time to catalog and summarize ... "

Lauren sent her memo to Human Resources under a nondescript cover. Not attempting to affect change in any sort of public or disruptive way, but attempting to affect change nonetheless. The immediate outcome of her document was immeasurable in all ways but one: she was pushed out of the company with a settlement and a nondisclosure agreement mere weeks later.[64]

In recent interviews, Lauren looks every bit the epitome of a young entertainment executive. She's polished, pretty, not overly made up. She wears black in a way that makes you think it might be her signature color. She smiles honestly when she talks about her work, very frank about how wonderful of an opportunity The Weinstein Company was.[65] And then the interview goes deeper, and her demeanor changes.

"You go to the systems, the small powers that be—not small, but the localized powers that be—that you think will be able to affect immediate change. You're often left wondering if any change occurs. You're also often silenced," she says,

---

64 Jodi Kantor and Megan Twohey, *She Said* (New York: Penguin Press, 2019), 142.

65 Lauren O'Connor, interview by Amy Goodman, *Democracy Now!* January 29, 2019.

speaking slower, with more pause. You can see her thinking. "The other path is, you know, it's public."[66]

But Lauren didn't choose to go public. Hers was a quiet departure, and soon after, she was hired as a Literary Development and Adaptation Executive at Amazon Studios (which is, arguably, a promotion).[67]

A year later, the New York Times' reporters had been working for months to gather enough publishable evidence to release a detrimental exposé. They were documenting the truth about the powerful producer Lauren had worked under, but there was a problem. The women who had decidedly left the producer unreported years before were not eager to go on the record now. If they had been hesitant to share an intimate story with a wide audience, then, an attribution in the New York Times was not exactly assuaging that fear now.[68]

And then the reporters—two driven and personable women in their own right—were slipped Lauren's memo by a senior executive at Weinstein. They had no choice but to include it. Lauren asked them not to use her name, but due to journalistic protocols, they could not grant her anonymity. Finally, complete with sourced evidence, the first of many stories on that producer went live. Lauren's full name was in the third paragraph.[69]

October 5, 2017: the day the Times published.[70] Lauren was getting a grilled cheese when her phone started buzzing.

---

66 Ibid.

67 Lauren O'Connor's LinkedIn profile, accessed February 19, 2021.

68 Jodi Kantor and Megan Twohey, She Said (New York: Penguin Press, 2019), 142.

69 Jodi Kantor and Megan Twohey, "Harvey Weinstein Paid off Sexual Harassment Accusers for Decades," New York Times, October 5, 2017.

70 Ibid.

For three years, despite having three different phone numbers, it hasn't stopped.[71]

Other people wake up to alarms. Lauren wakes up to multiple calls from news outlets. Other people have one, maybe two email addresses. Lauren has four.[72] Other people might dream about being famous. Lauren craves the privacy she once had.

"I felt like all control that I had over my own life was taken from me. I felt stripped of my right to privacy," she said in one interview. "I associate my name in print with a fear of retaliation ... [and] losing any sense of agency over the way you might be perceived in the world by strangers or people you know."[73]

Loss is a divider. It carves life into two parts: before and after. From that moment on, every memory exists on one side of the split. Either in the simpler before, or the more-difficult after.

For Lauren, the division is privacy. She can measure life in when she had it, and then when she didn't.

She can also measure it before and after she spent hundreds of thousands of dollars in legal fees, attempting to minimize her exposure and protect herself from the powerful producer. Before and after she shelled out even more for therapy, which she needed as a result of the mass media exposure. Her memories now exist in terms of before and after she went off all social media. Before, when she liked grilled cheese, and after, when she developed a distaste for it.[74]

---

71 Irin Carmon and Amelia Schonbek, "Was It Worth It?" *New York Magazine, The Cut,* September 30, 2019.

72 Ibid.

73 Ibid.

74 Ibid.

When Lauren's name went up in newsprint it wasn't tied to the words "the assaulted." Since she hadn't reported her own assault, but rather the mistreatment of others, there was no "victim" or "survivor" terminology thrown her way. But even just the label "whistleblower" was enough. She became "defined by a single instant," as she explains.

"[For] the rest of your life, every time you walk into a room, whether it's a business meeting, a first date, or making a new friend, you have to assume that that one moment of time in your life precedes you, that someone has already decided who you are," she says, speaking to the "after" side of her loss. [75]

Isla decided not to risk suffering that "after." Unreported, she is not defined by any moment, poignant loss of privacy, or term other than her own name. She controls when and how she shares her story—she controls whose eyes reflect sadness back into hers.

Because it's difficult enough when people you know look at you with their eyebrows raised, wondering how you'll ever be okay. But at least you get to choose who you tell—who you litmus test. To have strangers know your name and your sad story before they know you? That is another type of pain.

Watching Lauren in interviews, legs crossed, hands folded, I wonder if she gets tired talking about press. Am I imagining the way her mouth turns down?

"It's ironic," she says. "We're in a moment right now that is about consent. It's about ownership of voice. It's in direct protest to objectification. And yet, when you are made into

---

75   Lauren O'Connor, interview by Amy Goodman, *Democracy Now!* January 29, 2019.

a public figure, you risk being objectified all over again by a label. We forget how to see the human behind the headlines."[76]

Any label can be harmful when mass media repeatedly identifies you by it. Not only do you lose privacy and control over your own image, but you lose the opportunity to explain yourself to every person who reads your story. With no feasible way to contact every *New York Times* reader, for example, Lauren was at the mercy of the reporters to do her justice. Thankfully they did, but as for all the other outlets that picked it up? That's hard to track. And without that opportunity to tell her own story, she says, "you worry your intention will be questioned. You worry your credibility will be questioned."[77]

The press is not entirely responsible here. The *Times* team who broke the exposé and used Lauren's name did an excellent job in every sense: from uncovering each detail, to representing each woman (and even the powerful producer) fairly, to inciting important societal shifts. In her book, *Virgin and the Vamp*, Helen Benedict argued that extreme media coverage of rape perpetuates harmful stereotypes.[78] When I asked her about the more recent coverage of sexual assault, including the stories spun with Lauren's name, she said she saw some improvement.

"The recent coverage has taken the focus away from … 'What did she do to deserve this?' to … 'Why does he think he can get away with this?'" Benedict attested. And Lauren agrees. While her printed name and the subsequent loss of privacy upended her life, she does not blame the media. Instead, she says:

---

76 Ibid.

77 Irin Carmon and Amelia Schonbek, "Was It Worth It?" *New York Magazine, The Cut,* September 30, 2019.

78 Helen Benedict, *Virgin or Vamp: How the Press Covers Sex Crimes* (New York: Oxford University Press, 1992).

"What I'm angry about is that there isn't another way. There isn't a system in place. You speak up through localized channels, such as HR, and nothing is done. And nobody listens. And the only other avenue I've come to know is the press, which means mass exposure."[79]

*

Like the women in this book, Lauren is upset that the localized systems for reporting sexual violence are so often ineffective. Reports fizzle when they are left to the devices of those systems. Incendiary media coverage can fire otherwise-forgotten reports up again and create the change that the local systems neglected to—the Fourth Estate is meant to fix problems in that way. But at what cost?

For the person who reported, the cost is simply too high. Any cost is too high.

When Chanel Miller's story was snagged from the police reports, she was tormented by articles that ended with her assailant's best swim times and comments beneath them that tore her apart.

Why was she outside in a dress in the winter?

If she had a boyfriend why wasn't he there?

Not trying to blame the victim but something is wrong if you drink yourself to unconsciousness... [80]

When Dr. Christine Blasey Ford came forward after decades of going unreported, she only intended to write a

79 Irin Carmon and Amelia Schonbek, "Was It Worth It?" *New York Magazine, The Cut,* September 30, 2019.

80 Chanel Miller, *Know My Name* (New York: Viking Press, 2019), 49.

letter to the Senate Judiciary Committee to be "helpful."[81] But the media tracked her down.

"Reporters appeared at my home and at my job demanding information about this letter," she remembered. "They called my boss and coworkers and left me many messages, making it clear that my name would inevitably be released to the media."[82]

And, even though Christine hadn't wanted "to go the media route," when she eventually faced no other option, she paid a high price.[83]

Senator Feinstein summed up this failure best: "Our institutions have not progressed on how they treat women when they come forward. In essence, they are put on trial and forced to defend themselves, and often revictimized in the process."[84]

Revictimization: that was the ultimate cost of mass media exposure, when Christine reported a decades-old assault via a letter to the Senate. When Lauren reported assaults that hadn't even happened to her, via a discrete memo to The Weinstein Company HR department, the cost differed, but was still life altering. The barrage of press assaulted her to the point where she needed three different phone numbers, four different email addresses, and thousands of dollars' worth of therapy.

Why don't people report?

If Lauren did when she was assaulted, imagine what could have happened.

---

81 Alexandria Neason and Nausicaa Renner, "The Media Bullying of Christine Blasey Ford," Columbia Journalism Review, September 27, 2018.

82 Ibid.

83 Ibid.

84 Ibid.

That young, twenty-something Lauren, just hours after being violated. In some ways, she looks a lot like Isla the day after that fateful California drive. Like Christine Blasey, the morning after that summer party. Like me, at nineteen. When people have just suffered assault, they are at their most vulnerable. Can you imagine, at that point, risking reassault by the press? After having a choice taken from you, can you imagine volunteering to forfeit your next decision: who gets to know about it?

When what's needed most is a private space to heal, can you imagine your name in headlines?

No wonder we opt out.

TO WORK, GROW, AND BE RESPECTED

———

*"As women, we get harassed everywhere and we
don't feel compelled to report it because it's not
considered a reportable offense. We're expected to
put up with it; it's the cost of doing business."*

—ABBY ELLIS

Say what you will about Hollywood, it owns its reputation
as a fake place.

Fictional faces cover billboards up and down Sunset
Boulevard while characters stalk tourists on the Walk of
Fame. Plastic surgery businesses boom because people in LA
aren't two-faced, they're one, surgically-improved face. New
Hollywood hopefuls meditate on "Fake it 'til you make it,"
whispering the mantra to themselves and each other through
heavily filtered Instagram posts.

Beautiful, shameless, and fantastically artificial.

Most of the time it made me smile. The pure, manufactured betterment of it all. For a city that revolves around exporting made-up stories, fakeness fits.

Once, though, it made me cry tears of absolute amazement.

There are plenty of noses in Hollywood. Plenty of lips. More headshots than there are residents, probably. When those things are perfectly shaped or plumped or airbrushed, it's not exactly novel. But one thing Southern California doesn't have a lot of? Rain.

That afternoon, the rainfall glistened before it hit the ground. Heavy and full, every drop promised meaning. The water fell musically, starting slowly before painting the air. Its patter echoed around us, filling the entire space. Like it was performing the cliché, "raining buckets."

I'd seen rain before. Coastal Connecticut storms, bleak Boston blusters. I'd laughed and cried and kissed in the rain. Fell in love to it, fell in puddles during it. But I'd never seen rain like this and never felt so moved while watching it pour.

Of course, that was by design. The rain was glistening thanks to the handiwork of our lead lighting guy and the spotlight he rigged just so. The rain techs choreographed it and controlled its speed and intensity with an entire board of buttons. The water looked like it was coming down in buckets because, I reminded myself, it literally was falling from buckets in the sound stage rafters.

We were shooting an emotional scene that day. The actors recited somber lines, and the drizzle synced up with the first traces of tears in their eyes. As they cried, the rain picked up, the director glanced down at her notes, and the crew stood in silence, just outside the storm.

Dry and happy, we admired the liquid theatrics.

Most people lining the scene were pros. Older, wiser, and, as is sometimes synonymous in the film business, more jaded than I was. They each filled a role: director and producers, yes, but also a woman with big hair whose job was specifically to train and watch the on-camera dog; a bespectacled woman called the "baby wrangler," who held the infant actors until they were called to set; a man to monitor the actors' diction; an audio woman; and a narrow-chinned lady who made sure props were placed exactly where they should be.

My role as a production assistant was simply to be around when they needed me. To bring producers a new copy of the script when they lost theirs, to build playpens when the baby wrangler was busy, and to file the audio woman's vacation request correctly and give paperwork to her replacement. I often printed scripts until 2:00 a.m., hand-delivering them to each office before locking up the stage, so they were ready to go in the morning. My work was busy and less glamorous than my colleagues', but I was new to Hollywood, and moments like the manufactured rain made it magical.

I blinked away tears that were probably gratitude (but could have been exhaustion), as the rain reverbed through me. Before I could slip a video on my phone, a crew member stepped into the space next to me.

"*Huh.*" He acknowledged the rain without enthusiasm.

Not that I expected any. This crew member asked that we all refer to him as "Savage"—a request that would only fly on a Hollywood set, where the bosses have a long list of more pressing things to worry about, and there is no on-set HR department to question that nickname. I knew him only from delivering lunch, which was another part of my day-to-day: collect, place, and deliver lunch orders to twenty overworked production staff. Often, Savage would complain about a lack of mayonnaise or that they forgot the fucking bacon bits on his salad. Once, when he refused to eat, I asked my boss if I should go back. She rolled her eyes. He could deal with it.

So, when Savage approached, I was not looking to make conversation with him. In fact, my entire body eye-rolled in his presence. I mentally calculated how long I had to stand next to him before I could leave without being rude. I responded to his *Huh* with an *Amazing, right?* and checked my phone. Sixty more seconds of rain-watching should do it.

We were quiet for a bit, absorbed in the beautiful rumble of sound-stage rain.

"We should have a wet T-shirt contest," he said, looking at no one in particular. But I was the only one in earshot. Gross.

"Hah," I half-laughed, hoping it was enough of a neutral-sounding acknowledgment. It was time for me to go. I'd mumble an excuse about needing to check something and leave without creating the impression that I was completely repulsed by him.

"I'd like to see you in a wet T-shirt." Again, he spoke faced forward. This time, though, he side-eyed to see my reaction after.

It had been three years since that original assault, during my freshman year of college, introduced me to how inappropriate men could be, and I'd spent a solid portion of that time coming to terms with it. While I can't remember the specifics of my reaction—whether I coughed out another "hah" or choked on an "um" or fired back a "yeah, okay"—I know I wasn't shocked by his comment.

As much as I didn't want to leave the rain, I bolted to the golf cart parked outside and flew back to the production office. Bouncing around the lot, I considered my next move. Despite what his behavior might lead you to believe, he was much higher up on the glamour and power scale than I was.

I was new to Hollywood, but not naive.

I knew that if I pissed him off, he could have me fired, and the next person hoping to work in television would be at my desk the next day. He could advise his friends against hiring me on their shows. Sounds dramatic, but this is the stuff they feed Hollywood newcomers to get them to labor through just about anything. *"Reputation is everything in the film biz,"* they'd said. And now, I had to manage mine around his comment.

Reporting to any type of corporate, studio HR department, or even my boss, who took her job seriously and would speak to Savage, was out of the question. Instinctively, I knew it was my responsibility not to react. He was nasty—and not in the cool "nasty woman" sense. To protect myself, I had to forego any type of report.

It would mean protecting him.

But as I rounded the corner toward the office, I thought about a couple other people I could protect. My two female, mid-level coworkers. They were probably around thirty, shared an office, and interacted with Savage as often as I did. Without a functional system to shield them, I employed front porch methodology and shielded them myself.

"It wasn't that big of a deal," I said casually. *"But yeah, he's so gross."* I was processing out loud in their office, gauging their reactions. *"I don't really want to tell anyone besides you guys. But it was just creepy."*

They sang a chorus of anti-Savage remarks, but before I left, one of them opened a note on her computer.

"Wait, Kaley. What exactly did he say, again?"

*

Caught up in my first California summer and looking for my next job (the show with the fake rain wrapped in September), I forgot many details from those twelve-hour workdays spent between sound stages and the production office. I took care to itemize what I'd learned—what I could repeat in an interview to prove I wasn't completely green—and let the rest of it go. Production assistant work can be brutal: it's the hazing before you're accepted into the most elite fraternity in the world (a comparison that feels inherently negative anyway, considering how problematic fraternities are). Beyond the rain and sunny golf cart rides and kind restaurant owners who helped me sort through lunch orders, there wasn't much I wanted to remember.

Somehow, I worked my way onto the network side of TV. Just one month after my last day on set, I had a sweet boss, a lunch break, and a 9:00 a.m. to 6:00 p.m. schedule. The dress code required nicer outfits than jeans and a T-shirt, the office was pristine, and I was given a work laptop. The HR department led me through onboarding and assured my entire group of new hires that they were just downstairs, if we ever needed anything.

Sleeping and earning a lot more, I exhaled. I felt like I'd conquered Hollywood: Round One.

This network job looked like a two-year stint, at least. I had a lot to learn there and finally took a break from job hunting. So, when my phone rang one November evening, and it was the studio that produced the fake rain show, I let it ring for a beat. Was this an interview? I hadn't applied for a job there, had I? I applied to a lot of jobs during my first eleven months in Hollywood.

"*Hi, this is the studio HR department,*" they began. There were two women on the call. One would take notes—if that was okay with me. It was an interview, but they weren't looking to hire. They wanted to ask about my time working on the show.

As I coasted home from my new job, their voices blared through my Volkswagen Beetle sound system. This was part of an investigation, it was clear. But why would they include the most junior production assistant? Why did they care about my takes on the show, the executive producer, Savage? They asked about my experiences with him in particular. Did he ever do anything to make me uncomfortable?

"*I mean, he was a jerk about lunch orders. But nothing I couldn't handle. Everyone kind of knew he wasn't the nicest guy.*"

They pressed and pressed, looking for something. A born people pleaser, I overtalked, but could sense I wasn't giving them what they wanted. Then, forty-five minutes in, they came out with it: they received a report and needed to verify it. Did Savage ever make a specific comment, maybe about a contest, like a wet—

"*Oh. Right. Wow, this is just coming back to me, sorry.*" And it really was. "*Yeah, one time he said something about wanting to see ... me in a wet T-shirt.*"

Recounting the comment to those faceless voices was awkward. I imagined how they must be picturing me. Men didn't tell successful, serious professionals they'd like to see them in a wet T-shirt. I knew I lacked the success component—I was assigned to get his lunch, after all. But I strived to be serious and professional. My career in Hollywood was, at that point, my number one priority. I'd worked too hard to jeopardize it, which is why I hadn't reported in any more legitimate way than the inter-office warning.

The anger surprised me, but boy did it come. My name was on record with the studio now, in connection with this creepy guy, and I didn't have a choice in the matter. I imagined them firing him and listing the offenses: *"We received a complaint about a 'wet T-shirt contest.'"* "Sexual harassment," they'd call it. He would assume I made the complaint, that I'd wanted him punished.

In reality, I'd opted out of reporting. But now, the retaliation he could inflict on me would be the same as if I had.

I imagined applying for my next job. If it were at the studio, what would the HR department see when they pulled up my profile to vet me? Would there be a note: *involved in sexual harassment claim in 2017*? And if there was, wouldn't it be easy and valid to just move on to the next, less potentially problematic candidate?

I may have been operating under the influence of dark Hollywood lore—a power imbalance that will hopefully become outdated as society continues to reform itself. But the universality of my fear here is real. People work hard—often, too hard—to risk losing stature because of the repercussions of a report.

For a minute, I seethed at the mid-level employee who must have given my name and my story to these HR people without ever asking me. I didn't want to work under someone like Savage, I didn't want to have to figure out how to deal with comments like that during my first year of working (or ever), and I didn't want to be on the phone with studio HR, dragged into the case she'd built against him.

Control had been taken from me, and I was indignant. Savage made the comment to me, so I should get to handle it the way I chose to: to warn my coworkers, but not go on record with the HR department. For more than one reason,

I didn't think it was worth risking him being fired. He had a family, I was scared of retaliation, and, perhaps most of all, I couldn't spend the time dealing with a report when I was already so tired from printing scripts until 2:00 a.m.

The words of an older woman I'd met once echoed in my head: *I just wanted to work, grow, and be respected for the career I was building.*

And, of course, that's what the mid-level employee wanted too. To work and grow. She'd been in the industry ten years longer than I had. It wasn't hard to imagine the level of exasperation I might have with gross men after ten more years of having to work under them when I didn't respect them. I didn't blame her.

But I didn't want to report.

"*Look, I just want to be clear.*" I began, getting out of my head and back to the conversation with studio HR. "*I don't think he's a good person, but I was not so uncomfortable with his comment that I brought it to you myself. It took me this long to remember it, even. I think ...*" I stuttered. Did I think?

"*I think I'd feel bad if he got fired over this.*"

The HR team assured me that everything was confidential and they weren't taking any definitive action based on my story. It was just part of a larger report—they had many complaints against Savage. I hoped that, by the time I pulled onto my beachy Californian street and hung up the phone, I'd assured them that I was serious, professional, and thick-skinned enough to work in Hollywood. That I could deal with graphic comments and would not create HR headaches at the slightest slip of a wet T-shirt remark. I was hustling, had been hustling for eleven months, and didn't have time or patience for a gross, old guy to slow me down.

The college assault was bigger in every sense. Violating in ways that weren't just verbal. After the HR duo said goodbye, thanking me for taking the time to chat, I parallel parked and allowed myself to go back there for a minute. To that night in Boston, to the disjointed days after, and to the first time I was asked, *Why didn't you report?* Immobile in the driver's seat, exhausted from the uncertainty of the hour-long HR conversation, a response bounced through my head. It was bitter, but not untrue.

Because it would have felt like that, on steroids.

I continued moving forward, leaving Savage and the HR ladies and the coworker that reported for me behind—until I sat down to write this piece and got curious. Did Savage ever get fired, in the wake of the many complaints against him? Even though I didn't report willingly, a report was made.

Did it have an effect?

His professional biography is brimming with episodes, right up to the most recently released episode of that show with the fake rain. I had another bitter, not untrue thought.

Why bother risking your career, if things don't change, anyway?

And then another.

Thank god I didn't report in college.

NAOMI

I'd only met Naomi once, somewhat by chance, but her wise words centered me as I balanced the entire beginning part of my career: to work, to grow, and to be respected.

The day she showed me around the software start-up's office, I was nineteen. Awkwardly stuffed into a hand-me-down "business dress" and heels, I'd taken the train into the city for the day with my dad, who had the idea that it might be good for me to "experience the working world." His friend, an executive at the software company, was too busy to entertain me that morning. So, the responsibility landed with Naomi.

Immediately I wanted to be like her, channeling every bit of that intense admiration that's unique to nineteen-year-old girls. Her dark-olive skin blended to a cascading black mane, and nothing about her business look felt awkward or hand-me-down. She was ambitious, intelligent, and intentionally working her way up in the working world. Barely twenty-five, she found herself hustling alongside a predominantly male team at the start-up software company and shouldering the added weight of a toxic workplace during her hustle.

Naomi's story is similar to Lauren O'Connor's in many ways. Like Lauren, her drive led her to a turbo-charged position at a young age. Like Lauren, she worked in a space that sexual harassment owned. And, like Lauren, she crafted a memo detailing everything she saw at The Company. The mirror warps, however, when it comes to reporting. There, Naomi becomes Lauren's inverse. She never emailed her document under an innocuous subject line—she never sent it to even the most localized channels. She's unreported.

But I didn't know any of that on the day I toured her office.

The booths at underground city cafés are especially conducive to secret-sharing. After traipsing the entire length of the trendy workspace, we took a lunch break there. Naomi leaned in when she spoke to me, thick hair tied back in a neat ponytail and perfectly manicured nails tapping the phone screen in front of her. She had the golden confidence of a mid-twenties woman who had already encountered success, and when she spoke, the confidence caught. Everything about her was contagious.

"I made a bucket list for myself when I turned twenty," she said in a tone that could only be categorized as somewhere

between gushing and matter-of-fact. The assumption was that any successful person would have made the same list. *"On there, I wrote 'work for a start-up.' So here I am!"*

She went on, passionately discussing life and professionalism, and it was obvious I was sharing a booth with someone who knew how to be in charge in an effective way. Smart, sweet, and sure. She spoke with conviction.

But I'll never forget the undertone of disappointment in her voice. The subtle scan of the café she did before lowering her voice over that soup/salad combo. She hadn't quite gotten what she'd hoped for, she confessed. Sure, maybe no one does at a start-up. But it was more than that.

Naomi graduated from college ready to work, and just a year into her first high-powered position, she decided to shift her career. Feeling unfulfilled in the publishing world, she fearlessly made a career switch, working instead for big-name IT companies. Despite IT being a notoriously male-dominated field, she was a junior project manager in no time, and it was widely anticipated that she'd keep climbing, fast. But the bucket list item tugged at her heart, and in a second boldly authentic move, she took a job at the start-up software company just before her birthday.

The space was enchanting—designed to attract smart people like Naomi. With floor-to-ceiling windows and brand-new design features, The Company boasted an open-office floor plan before it was widely adopted at every other sleek up-and-comer. They had a fully stocked bar, kombucha on tap, and the employees wore jeans on days other than just Friday. But, even after just a morning there, I suspected something less progressive behind the scenes.

It had something to do with the way the men there spoke to me, or the way they looked at each other.

Naomi's café confessional confirmed it. Sketchy things were happening at this company. Sexual harassment, inappropriate mixing of business and pleasure, drug-fueled parties in the open-floor-plan office. There was enough to fill up more than just a lengthy memo, it was clear. I'd psyched myself up for a day in the "adult" world, but the more I learned, the more deeply I was struck by how un-adult this all seemed. Without actually asking anything of Naomi, I was sure my eyes gave me away as I questioned everything.

Was I hearing this right? And, if so, was this what I had to look forward to?

Years before I had my own experience in Hollywood, I considered: *Were any of my dreams big enough to keep me working in TV, another notoriously male-dominated field?*

Naomi whispered words I didn't understand at the time. Words I was pretty sure weren't supposed to be understood by a person with just two semesters of college under her belt—big, legal terms that sounded notorious. She detailed how she'd been brought on with a slew of promises, about how she accepted a job to help manage this company, but how that wasn't quite coming to fruition.

The Friday before, she told me, the CEO called an all-staff meeting. The Company had secured a new deal of some sort, and everyone raised a glass of champagne. He gave a speech, listing thorough personal thanks, running through employees at all levels, naming those who had made this happen. He used words like *buddy* and *the man* and *dude*. It was the type of speech anyone working fifty-to-sixty-hour weeks wanted to be included in. Naomi wasn't thanked.

The sexism was the least of it. There was so much more, she said, that she couldn't tell me.

Here's the thing about that kind of blatant sexism: it doesn't always indicate the presence of more sinister happenings. But, when rumors about sexual misconduct come out, it does make them a lot more believable.

Naomi stayed with The Company until the bitter end. She was there when the rumors became news, and when the news became widespread. I clicked through the articles from my parent's house. I was grateful I'd only spent a day in that office, but also, vaguely anxious about how many more of those days I might have ahead of me.

She was there when that thankless CEO declined to comment on the rumors, and she was there when he quit, days later, "to pursue other career opportunities." She watched as other employees left soon after with settlements.

Naomi, nothing if not loyal, was there when the new management asked anyone who had complaints about the ex-CEO to come forward. She had her memo at the ready. But then—

"All the guys knew what was going on, but no one stood up or did anything," she says, years later. "You feel like you'd be a whistleblower. Like you can't hang. And plus, I realized, who would I be giving that document to?" There was never a reliable Human Resources department to report to at The Company, but even if there had been, they'd all left with settlements earlier that fall.

"I wasn't looking to bring down a company and I wasn't looking to humiliate someone," Naomi adds.

"I got to a point where I think it just wasn't worth it for me ... all I want to do at any company is work, grow, and be respected for who I am in my job."

I learned a lot from Naomi, in that formative day I spent with her. That intention was perhaps the most important.

Naomi was at the start-up for just under four years. Eventually the company went bankrupt, costing both investors and employees millions.

In the first six months after Naomi left the work environment that was riddled with sexual misconduct, she got her two-hundred-hour yoga certification, bought a one-way ticket to a new city, and then moved cross-country to resume her career. She now works as a high-power executive at a large software company, speaking on panels and winning awards at every turn, and she's "not taking shit from anyone, this time around."

"Sometimes I still wonder if I made the right decision. But I felt like I handled myself in a way that was honest and respectful and, well, the media is a really scary place. The last thing I'd ever want to do is, like, expose myself to that."

OLIVIA

Olivia Garrett raised her hand against a powerful man.

At first, she raised it quietly, just barely over her head. She made a point not to interrupt anyone—including the freshman lawmaker who groped her.

She was twenty-three, fresh out of college, and working as a legislative aide in Alaska.[85] It's easy to picture her, decked in a blazer and glasses, walking through the golden State Capital doors into the very regal, very marble lobby. Life might have felt glamorous, rushing through lavish blue carpeted hallways, passing framed relics, attending important meetings. And life must have felt confusing, when, in one of those hallways,

---

85 Nathaniel Herz, Julia O'Malley, "Seven Aides at Alaska Capitol Say Legislator Made Unwanted Advances and Comments," *Anchorage Daily News*, December 8, 2017.

a first-term lawmaker grabbed her by the arm and told her that her haircut "turned him on."[86]

After that first comment, on January 16, 2017, she went unreported.[87]

"It was really gross and just kind of strange because he's an almost sixty-year-old man," Olivia later said in a phone interview with a local radio station.[88] "So I just kept kind of walking because I wasn't really sure what to do about it."

She had a pixie cut, a job to do, and now, a colleague to ignore. He had other plans.

Less than two months later, in a crowded room, that same Democratic representative grabbed Olivia's butt as he walked by her. Organized and precise, as you might expect a person who lands a legislative aide gig to be, she began the formal process of raising her hand and submitted her official report two days later.[89]

The letter, dated March 13, 2017, began: "Dear Speaker Edgmon and Representative Tuck." The next twelve succinct sentences outline the incidents, and then the document wraps up with: "I am making you both aware so that you can share this with [the lawmaker] privately so no one is embarrassed or damaged."[90]

This is going to the local powers that be. The Human Resource-esque, noncriminal-justice, internal avenues. The

---

86 Olivia Garrett, letter to Representative Bryce Edgmon and Representative Chris Tuck, March 13, 2017.

87 Ibid.

88 Kyle Hopkins, "'He Should Resign. It's That Simple.' Woman Who Says She Was Groped by Alaska Lawmaker Says Apology Is Not Enough," *KTUU*, December 8, 2017.

89 Olivia Garrett, letter to Representative Bryce Edgmon and Representative Chris Tuck, March 13, 2017.

90 Ibid.

ones Lauren trusted. This is raising your hand against a powerful man, while remaining the polite, female, junior staffer that society and your coworkers expect you to be.

This letter received no response.

At least, none that Olivia noticed or was notified about.[91] So after eight months of holding her hand in the air, she stopped waiting to be called on and stood up. With the unanswered letter behind her, she threw down both hands and reported to the next great power she could think of. The one that Naomi avoided. Olivia spoke to the press.[92]

After Olivia marched bravely into the Fourth Estate, six other women followed. Six other staffers cited lingering hugs, sexual comments, and inappropriate touching from the same freshman, Democratic lawmaker who groped Olivia. Four of the incidents occurred after she submitted the letter.[93] While Olivia's hand was in the air, waiting to be called on, that lawmaker's hands kept moving, unrestrained, unmonitored.

When Olivia went public, she stopped working for the legislature. On some level, she knew her state job could not coexist with the justice she wanted.

"I did really like working for the legislature," she said, in an interview.[94] When she speaks, she sounds determined, but also vulnerable. Like a woman fighting for something

91 Irin Carmon and Amelia Schonbek, "Was It Worth It?" *New York Magazine, The Cut,* September 30, 2019.

92 Nathaniel Herz, Julia O'Malley, "Seven Aides at Alaska Capitol Say Legislator Made Unwanted Advances and Comments," *Anchorage Daily News,* December 8, 2017.

93 Ibid.

94 Kyle Hopkins, "'He Should Resign. It's That Simple.' Woman Who Says She Was Groped by Alaska Lawmaker Says Apology Is Not Enough," *KTUU,* December 8, 2017.

much bigger than herself. "I thought maybe at some point it was something I'd do again, but this is an epidemic ... and so I decided that it was time."

Something was taken from Olivia when that creepy lawmaker grabbed her. She lost the simple decision that she is entitled to make: whether or not she wanted him to. And then, in her quest to make things right, she gave up something else: her political career. The other six women who came forward in her wake did not opt for the second loss. As a local newspaper reported at the time, they "asked not to be identified out of fear of attracting attention to themselves in jobs in which discretion is prized."[95]

"Many of the women worried that speaking publicly about [the lawmaker] would damage their reputations," continued the newspaper, putting a truth that we all intuit into newsprint, "and make it harder to get work from other elected officials in the future."[96]

Were they correct in their worry? In Olivia's words, yes.

"It's pretty much impossible for me to find political work here," she told *The Cut*. After reporting to the press, she says, "other Democrats I've worked with before wouldn't look at me, wouldn't talk to me. Candidates will not pick me out to work on their campaigns. People stop including you in things or stop asking you for strategic advice. It's worth it, don't get me wrong. But isolation is a really powerful tool."[97]

We all know what it means to be isolated. It's the lack of that "we all." Shameful and immobilizing, isolation feels

---

95 Nathaniel Herz, Julia O'Malley, "Seven Aides at Alaska Capitol Say Legislator Made Unwanted Advances and Comments," *Anchorage Daily News*, December 8, 2017.

96 Ibid.

97 Irin Carmon and Amelia Schonbek, "Was It Worth It?" *New York Magazine, The Cut*, September 30, 2019.

like a slow sting—the painful belief and ever-deepening hurt that maybe we don't actually belong. Cold and disconnected, isolation is the opposite of the front porch. It's not a place where stories are shared, trust is implicit, and unconditional welcome reigns. It's not a place where progress is made, or solutions are found. And maybe that's by design.

Olivia now works in an organization that probably feels like isolation's inverse: the YWCA, as the Women's Economic Empowerment Program Manager. She continues aiding women, creating change at local levels. Her political career, though, is over.

So, why don't people report?

To save their careers.

GUILT AND SPACES

———

"We force her to think hard about what this will mean for his life, even though he never considered what his actions would do to her."

—CHANEL MILLER

TWO STORIES IN WHICH WOMEN ARE VIOLENT

ONE

People don't often run from consensual sexual encounters.

The night it happened to me, I shoved hard enough to land him on the floor and ran out. I didn't know what to call the experience then. Even now, my stomach tightens when I stumble through labelling it.

I could hear him shouting behind me but didn't care to make out what he was saying. *Get away, just get away* blared through my head, drowning everything else out.

Including my friend's calls to me. I ran into her in the foyer.

"Kale! Thank god. We were looking for you. Are you—"

"Brit! I'll explain but right now can we—"

"There's a Lyft outside. Mich and Lina are already in it."

Brit had my hand. We fell over ourselves and each other, down the steps and out the door. Before it could swing completely shut, he propelled it back to its hinge. We spilled into the car, trying to communicate in shouted half sentences. Everyone knew something was wrong. No one, except me, knew what. He was at the bottom step now, coming toward the car. Screaming *"What the fuck?"* or something like that.

"Close the door!" I pleaded, over the packed-sedan pandemonium. The way I remember it, this string of moments was pure cacophony.

But then he stuck his head into the car, and it all goes silent. I saw his angry mouth moving, spewing something drunk and intimidating, I'm sure, but couldn't hear the words. I pressed my face into Lina's shoulder, and someone pushed him out of the car door. Our Lyft sped away. I was shaking.

So this is it, I remember thinking. Even tipsy and fewer than ten minutes removed, I knew. *This is what happens to so many of us.*

Thank god mine wasn't worse.

TWO (SEVEN MONTHS LATER)

"You tried to punch him in the neck? Oh my god. Okay. Let's just leave."

Michelle was the fiercest friend I'd ever had. We tripped into each other's arms as clueless college freshmen, both freshly minted sorority girls. We questioned everything about the Greek-lettered experience aloud in each other's dorm rooms: What was appropriate mixer attire? How early should we get there? How did we wiggle our way into this sorority? Did we like it or hate it?

By the next year, we had more answers than questions. We tied a string of friends together, and she became the most loyal and uninhibited link. Tonight, she was also one of the drunkest.

I tugged Brit and Lina out of the bathroom line. *"Can we leave? Now? Michelle—"*

They didn't hesitate. Last time we "needed to leave" a party at this particular frat, we'd been chased out.

No time for goodbyes, we hoisted ourselves out of the basement, away from blaring lights and roaring boys. Boston's winter sting whipped around our bare legs, and Michelle yelled at it. She was fired up—to other buzzed partygoers on the street, she looked mad about everything. We knew it was really just one thing. The same one thing we were all always mad about.

The corner Tasty Burger, just ahead, glowed: shelter and carbs. Space to be angry.

"He came too close to me," she spat, between fries. *"And I just kind of mumbled that I knew what he did."*

She looked at me. Big, brown, apologetic eyes. They weren't sorry for erupting on him. They were sorry that even an attempted neck-punch wouldn't undo anything.

"He said, 'What did you just say?' And got up in my face." I could picture it too clearly. *"And then he kept asking and I just smiled at him and wouldn't say anything."* She pushed the fries toward me. *"Have some."*

I wondered what my expression had given away.

"But he wouldn't stop so, finally, I just said it. 'You raped my friend.'"

All three sets of eyes were on me now. Something dropped in my very-full stomach. She used the word. *Rape.* In the seven months since he ignored my first, second, third, fourth, fifth, sixth, seventh, "no," I hadn't spoken that word. A friend said it to me, once, but I never echoed it. That word implied dark alleys and bruises and screams, none of which appeared in my story.

Women aren't supposed to be violent. We're not supposed to accuse or explode. We're taught instead to empathize, to soften, to think through with grace. By referring to it as "assault," I took the edge off rape. Made it sound mild, blurry, like something I could make sense out of.

But did it make sense, that a summer and a semester later, I still got nervous every time our sorority mixed with his frat? I avoided the first few parties, opting out to the tune of confused friends. *"But Kaley, it's fourth of July themed! Your favorite!"* (embarrassing, but undeniable). I called it "assault" when I explained it to them for the first time, and then "you know, the thing" when I referenced it after that. *"I'm not a fan of that frat, remember? You know … the thing."*

Rape is a loud word.

The volume of your voice doesn't matter: people react to the four-letter word as if you screeched it. So I didn't call it rape, and it was easier to stay soft. But it wasn't any easier to make sense out of.

Part of me admired Michelle's disdain for the rules of being a girl. She often exploded, at a high volume, at men. I wasn't the only one of her friends who had been … assaulted. But the other part of me jumped to concern.

"Mich! You just straight up said that? Did you—" I bit my lip. The last thing I wanted was for her to think her brazen show of support was unappreciated. Gently, eyes on the linoleum counter between us, I asked. *"How loud did you say it?"*

She was drunk and unbothered and wouldn't turn on me. *"Oh, I just said it reallllll casually. And then of course he started shouting."*

It would've been possible, if not easy, to pass Michelle off as an angry, "crazy," drunk girl. An expression used to describe women all the time. But there was something about the way the frat boy heard what she said. The way he aggressively questioned Mich.

"*Wait, who?*" he'd badgered her. When she wouldn't tell him, he got angry. Closed in on her, demanding, just under the beat of the music, "*Who? Tell me!*"

Like he needed a name. People don't push so hard for the truth, if they know it isn't there.

She smirked and ignored him, until he finally cut the questions and articulated his rage.

"*Look. I'm going to be a very, very successful businessman. Okay? I don't need someone coming after me for money or something in twenty years. So why don't you just—*"

She lunged at him, throwing words like "selfish" and "unbelievable" and, apparently, a fist. The bystander who dragged her away from him said she was going for his neck.

That frat-party night left me with a couple things, beyond just a half-finished milkshake and a few leftover fries. One: Mich embodied a layer of anger that I wasn't sure I had. That ability—or was it freedom?—to get wildly loud and physical in defense of a friend. I couldn't, even for myself. Seven months before, all I could muster was a hard shove and an absolutely vicious, *I said no*, as I ran out the door. As violated and upset as I was, even now, I couldn't summon a reaction much stronger than avoiding him at parties.

But was I born without that ability, or raised without it?

And, two: the frat boy's primary concern was not whether or not he hurt someone. He didn't fumble Mich's accusation, asking what she meant or how someone could say something like that about him. He didn't claim it wasn't in his character—*I would never*—or ask to speak to me to understand what I meant. His first concern did not seem to be whether or not he fucked up my life. It was whether "someone" could fuck up his. In twenty years. Monetarily.

In the Lyft ride on the way home from Tasty Burger, speeding down an icy Commonwealth Avenue, I shook my head and laughed, almost, as I thought back to those hot summer hours and days after. When I decided to leave him unreported. When I'd reasoned that ignoring my "no" wasn't enough for me to potentially wreck his life. He attended an elite university, was an athlete there. Even though he'd taken something from me (what, exactly, I still wasn't sure), I would feel guilty taking a future from him. I didn't ask for the power he'd given me, and I wasn't going to use it.

Was I born with that conscience, or raised with it?

Either way, I knew his alcohol-fueled fit about *someone* and *money or something* was misplaced. I would never need his money. And I'd never come for him. Because as important as he was sure that he was going to be, this wasn't about him.

I didn't report because, yes, I would have felt guilty if he were punished in an irreparable way. But also, I didn't report because I needed it to be about me. My ignored words, my healing, the rest of my life, beyond that night. I was already questioning so much. I didn't want to have to question whether or not he deserved whatever punishment came his way, if I reported.

Or, worse, if the system failed to react at all, I didn't want to question why a punishment never came his way. He had to live with an attempted neck punch and the knowledge that "someone" could come after him. That felt like the option that more surely enforced the type of justice I wanted. That felt like part of the control I'd lost.

So, I left it there. Hoping he carried the guilt. Sure that I never would.

RACHEL

Rachel had to share a locker, which was a huge bummer. But it was only kindergarten.

I was never told to share a locker, but in middle school, we were dying to. You scribbled your three-number combo on a scrap of paper and slid it into your best friend's palm, and then somewhere between the layers of stickers that filled that three-by-one-foot cube, your friendship was forever. It was one of those preteen phases that, when you peel away glitter and braces, speaks to a life truth. Inviting someone to share your space is sacred. Cohabiting, even in a metal cube, connects people.

So, Rachel had to share a locker in kindergarten, and it was with a boy. They were connected not by choice, but by cohabitation. Sometime between the beginning of their bond as locker-mates and middle school, though, she deduced that he wanted to share more than just a three-digit combo.

Locker-mate had a crush on her; as anyone who has either been or interacted with a boy at that age knows, it's usually not hard to tell. Chasing the object of your desire around the playground isn't exactly subtle. That signature teasing-one-day, love-note-the-next dichotomy can be head-spinning, but it also gives a person away. Despite their evidence, Rachel never reciprocated his feelings. And as the duo grew further away from the playground-chasing phase, they grew into an authentic friendship.

Authentic friendship is always crucial. But it's especially crucial when you leave your rural hometown, a small Jewish community, and begin the overwhelming chaos that is freshman year at a city university.

It's difficult to imagine a more universally upside-down time than that first semester of college. No matter how many pamphlets you read or older kids you follow on social media, almost no one is ready to suddenly uproot the life they've known for eighteen years and start over, sleeping and dressing and sharing space with a complete stranger. In that insane uncertainty, you survive both by making random bonds and strengthening the ones you already have. That girl with the sweet Southern accent on your floor? You're best friends, inseparable and thriving. That authentic friend, the one you've known since kindergarten, who ended up at a college just minutes away? You have more in common now than ever before.

You're unsure of everything, open-minded to anything, and hyperaware of the beautiful and terrifying opportunity you have to create your life away from home. So, when that authentic friend and former locker-mate invites you to his frat party, you float it in the group chat with your new girlfriends. You feel relieved when they seem excited to go.

Rachel and her first-semester freshman crew traipsed to a couple of locker-mate's parties. They were sweaty (any US city in September), and crowded (so many freshmen girls bonding with friends, and so many freshmen boys trying to impress upperclassmen with all the girls they could bring). Those parties felt and tasted and beat like college. A sure sign they were on the right path to a memorable private-university experience.

By October, the big invite came. A themed party, and not just any theme. "The Catalina Wine Mixer Party."[98] Locker-mate's frat was famous—or, depending on how you looked at it, infamous—for it.

---

98 Adam McKay, *Step Brothers*. (Los Angeles, CA: Sony Pictures Releasing, 2008).

It's the fucking Catalina Wine Mixer.[99]

The movie *Step Brothers* made the line legendary, and then fraternities nationwide made it a reality. Dress in head-to-toe prep, carry a plastic wine glass, and celebrate with dormmates and "the brothers" while everyone lovingly quotes the movie—"Did we just become best friends?"—but no one nails it quite like Will Ferrell did. [100]

How awesomely pure it is to be able to debate which plaid skirt is hotter without wondering if it's putting you in danger. To drape fake pearls over a tube top and giggle, not feeling like you need to cover up. To watch as boys take shots and chug the fuchsia juice, scooped from a bucket, and to fearlessly do the same.

Rachel did, and it's the last thing she remembers. She invited the vat-juice, as it was ominously called, to slide down her throat, and she is almost positive she was roofied in some capacity.

Rohypnol drugs (roofies, for short) aren't made to take you out of your mind, but when mixed with alcohol, they do. Xanax also does the trick. Even a drug-free jungle juice, which is most often just a mix of fruit juices and different alcohols, including 190-proof Everclear, can transport you places you wouldn't normally go. Literally and figuratively.

For Rachel, it was literal. She ended up upstairs in the frat, rolling around on the floor. Her friends of one month wanted to leave and did so without her—it's less hard to leave a person behind when you barely know them. Plus, they must have reasoned, her locker-mate from forever ago assured them he would take care of her.

---

99 Ibid.
100 Ibid.

The next morning, Rachel woke up with a blurry memory. The kind that's impossible to make out in motion, but a few individual frames were clear. Concentrating, she watched the fast-forwarded movie and landed, for a second, on different scenes. She was in locker-mate's dorm. She was being pushed against a bed. He was inside of her. Was he inside of her? How did she get home? She fell back asleep, fake pearls long gone.

Rachel's voice is sweet and almost sing-songy, exuding confidence and honesty. "In some ways that's very fortunate that I don't totally remember what happened, because then I don't have to relive it," she considers, for a beat. "I have friends that were awake during theirs, and I think that's a lot more traumatizing."

Theirs. What happens to so many of us.

While she didn't have much of a memory, she did have a muddy tube top and a weird feeling about the few scenes she could recall.

Rachel didn't come out of her room the entire weekend after "The Famous (or Infamous) Catalina Wine Mixer" party.[101] From the safety of her twin XL, she called her aunt.

"Do you think you had sex?" her aunt asked.

"I'm not sure, I think so."

"You would know for sure if you did."

Silence. Rachel thought back on the fragmented scene. Was he inside of her?

"Well, if you don't know for sure, just ask him to make sure he's clean. You don't want to report or anything, right?"

And then it was set. The unreport, sealed.

"I was like, I don't want to ruin his life," Rachel says now, looking back. "I just want this to not be a thing."

---

101 Ibid.

Thinking about her reasons for not reporting at the time, she continues. "I know a lot of times charges like this aren't taken seriously. But if they were, and this were to really be prosecuted, it would've had a huge effect on my hometown. Plus, he was in ROTC (Reserve Officers' Training Corps) in college, and I was really worried about ruining his life or taking away his scholarship. I knew those things would have been affected. I knew he couldn't afford school without that scholarship."

She pauses, and then concludes, "I was more worried about how it would affect him than how it affected me."

Was Rachel born with that conscience, or was she raised with it?

Rachel and locker-mate shared a metal cube at age five, but they always shared more than that. A hometown, a small Jewish community. Those spaces are sacred. They connect people.

Of course, it was different after that night. Post-Catalina Wine Mixer, they shared another space. One that Rachel hadn't invited him into.

Rachel stopped responding to his party invites. She barely spoke to him again, actually, and their authentic friendship dissolved under the weight of what she doesn't totally remember but didn't at all consent to. By sophomore year, she found a new group of friends, forging bonds that went deeper than one month. That year, as any suburban town would have it, she ran into locker-mate at a hometown bar on Thanksgiving Eve.

"Every once in a blue moon, something sparks me," she says. That night, she sparked. "I flipped out."

Months later, Rachel and locker-mate had another encounter. She was home again and saw him while at a restaurant with her family. Their parents are friendly.

"It was really awkward," she remembers. "It would've been even more awkward if there was legality involved. I mean, we literally shared a locker in kindergarten. I grew up with him."

The further Rachel grew away from locker-mate, the steadier she became. Hometown run-ins became less frequent, and her thoughts about that night did too. Although she became less consciously aware of the impact "The Catalina Wine Mixer" had on her day-to-day life, her unconscious didn't let go as quickly.[102] She says it took her years to stop picking toxic relationships, first on her own and then with the help of a therapist. She processed and learned and slowly figured out "how to not feel useless." For a while, she had a hard time connecting and a hard time not faulting herself.

Why would I ever have that drink?

Why would I ever go to that party?

Why would I ever spend time with people who would just leave me?

But now, Rachel's rounding out her graduate degree at a premier university, on the brink of a bold career pivot into teaching. She's tackling a major city, and even though her space is small, she's invited someone to share it with her. She's cohabiting and connecting. For four and a half years, she's been in a relationship with a man she describes as "very stable and healthy, and so supportive."

There was only one time that her current boyfriend was even slightly less than understanding. Her high school reunion was approaching, and she refused to go. He pushed her—it would be fun and he could come or not come depending on what she wanted, but this was one of those things. You can't miss out on your high school reunion.

---

102 Ibid.

"But then I just dropped the, 'A kid in my high school class raped me' line, just really spelled it out for him," she says with that signature good-humored confidence. "That was effective."

She didn't go to the reunion. And she's not sure if locker-mate went either. What she does know is that he works in the navy now, having graduated his ROTC program and private university years ago. He lives on base with his wife.

"I don't know that he identifies it as rape. He probably thinks, 'Oh, she was drunk, whatever, fine. I was drinking too.' But ..." Rachel trails off. Maybe lost in the juxtaposition of how sharing a space can either make or break a relationship, depending on how that space is respected.

LINDSAY

It was a man's world. Lindsay broke in with a pair of leggings.

Athletic wear, to be specific—or, as the market would call it, "athleisure." A twenty-eight-year-old female entrepreneur with a background in the wellness and healthcare arenas, Lindsay Meyer was made to harness the trend. As biker shorts and track suits were just catching on with consumers, she launched an innovative way to buy them: Active Collective, which is the first and only athleisure trade show in the United States. On both the East and West Coasts, her company showcases over 250 brands and draws crowds of thousands.[103]

But Lindsay's story isn't about sports bra sales. It's about existing in a world that isn't meant for you. It's about the survival instincts that existence demands.

---

103 "Why Attend," Active Collective, accessed February 19, 2021.

Lindsay is San Francisco-based and epitomizes the cool-business ease that the venture capital industry is known for. She graduated Notre Dame a year early with an interdisciplinary degree and wasted no time before beginning to build her entrepreneurial resume.[104] She must have moved with stunning focus and dexterity; walking San Francisco's steep streets is exhausting, but no match for climbing its start-up ecosystem.

You know those moments when you stop, and really feel the place in which you're living? When you realize how the community spins and see your spot in its turn?

I wonder what it was like for Lindsay the first time she had one of those moments. When she saw herself, not in the San Francisco hills or the venture capitalism ecosystem, but in a man's world. It's one thing to recite a statistic—in 2016, female entrepreneurs received $1.5 billion in funding versus $58.2 billion for men, for example—but it's another to actually experience the reality and your place in it.[105]

Given the world she'd landed in, it must have felt especially empowering when, in 2015, Lindsay secured a $25,000 investment from a venture capitalist. Not just any venture capitalist either—a "well connected Silicon Valley venture capitalist," as *The Information* later referred to him.[106] He used his own money to invest and came on board just as Active Collective was starting to take off. His interest was valuable and to a younger, less experienced entrepreneur could have been validating.

And then he took a different type of interest.

---

104 Lindsay Meyer, LinkedIn profile, accessed February 19, 2021.

105 Axios, "Talk of Tech: Women Reveal Silicon Valley's Sexism," *Axios*, July 1, 2017.

106 Reed Albergotti, "Silicon Valley Women Tell of VC's Unwanted Advances," *The Information*, June 22, 2017.

First, the texts began rolling in. *Was she attracted to him? Would she rather be with him than her boyfriend?*[107] She was busy climbing, creating, working, and weird texts weren't about to get in her way—not when nothing else had. I imagine her grimly thinking it was the price of admission—survival instincts for existing in a man's world.

Then he groped her and kissed her, and Lindsay's survival instinct leveled up. The price of admission was draining, but this felt like a bigger bill. She reported her discomfort to a mentor, who alerted the well-connected venture capitalist's company. Nothing changed. "I felt like I had to tolerate it because this is the cost of being a nonwhite female founder," Lindsay later told the *New York Times*.[108]

She's Asian American, with long, thick, black hair. She speaks clearly, enunciating every word. Sometimes, in interviews, her hair falls into a curl at the end. Sometimes, in interviews, her sentence falls into an emotional break at the end.

For a long time, Lindsay opted out of giving any interviews. She tolerated and talked through the harassment with her mom, a couple friends, and a coworker.[109] She left Active Collective by the end of 2015. A news outlet began investigating the well-connected venture capitalist, piecing together reports of his "unwanted advances" from many women.[110]

But Lindsay remained reticent to go on the record. "I was launching my next start-up," she told *New York Magazine*. "I

---

107 Katie Benner, "Women in Tech Speak Frankly on Culture of Harassment," *The New York Times,* June 30, 2017.

108 Ibid.

109 Irin Carmon and Amelia Schonbek, "Was It Worth It?" *New York Magazine, The Cut,* September 30, 2019.

110 Reed Albergotti, "Silicon Valley Women Tell of VC's Unwanted Advances," *The Information,* June 22, 2017.

decided it wasn't worth ... what I assumed would be tarnishing my professional reputation by going public with this."[111]

A year and a half later, *The Information* published their exposé: six tech-industry women accused the venture capitalist of "unwanted, inappropriate advances."[112] Many of them remembered that the advances came while they were trying to secure funding and launch their businesses—when they were in peak survival mode in a man's world.

Initially, Lindsay struggled with the decision to add her name to the list of accusers.

But after considering what would happen if her story got out and she hadn't been the one to tell it, she decided to publicly corroborate. The Saturday after *The Information* broke their piece, Lindsay emailed a *New York Times* reporter with her number.[113] By the end of that month, her story found its place in the final paragraph of the *New York Times'* piece, "Women in Tech Speak Frankly on Culture of Harassment."[114]

The well-connected venture capitalist responded with the cool business-ease that's signature to his industry, but not at all appropriate in this situation. In the first statement he released, he denied the allegations. Then, in his second statement, he was "disturbed" by them. Pressure mounted, and he resigned from his prestigious position at a venture

111 Irin Carmon and Amelia Schonbek, "Was It Worth It?" *New York Magazine, The Cut,* September 30, 2019.

112 Reed Albergotti, "Silicon Valley Women Tell of VC's Unwanted Advances," *The Information,* June 22, 2017.

113 Irin Carmon and Amelia Schonbek, "Was It Worth It?" *New York Magazine, The Cut,* September 30, 2019.

114 Katie Benner, "Women in Tech Speak Frankly on Culture of Harassment," *The New York Times,* June 30, 2017.

capital firm. He updated his LinkedIn: "Head of Self-Reflection, Accountability & Change," it read.[115]

Venture capitalism might be a man's world, but the venture capitalist that groped Lindsay had just undone his own place in it.

For Lindsay, the aftermath of reporting to the press looked less linear. After Active Collective, she did some consulting and finished launching that next start-up. Her LinkedIn has been updated quite a few times: today, it reads, "CEO." In her own words, she is "definitely more of a public figure these days"—and not because of her work.[116] In 2017, *TIME* included her in their "person of the year" feature, The Silence Breakers.[117] She recognizes that this public platform gives her "the ability to educate and inspire others," but even so, she says, "If I had known what I would have to endure, I'm not sure I would have gotten to this place."[118]

Just to survive, Lindsay endured harassment, assault, the barrage of media inquiry that comes with reporting to the press. She managed her emotions around each of those trials expertly—both the coverage and her continued success speak to that. But there was another, less talked-about emotion that tugged at her.

"He never got in touch with me," she remembered. "I think that he and his family probably suffered a lot. Enough, even. I am 500 percent cognizant that my experiences and the way I presented them to reporters who shared them with the

115 Ryan Mac, "Disgraced Venture Capitalist Justin Caldbeck Threatened Legal Action against One of His Accusers," *Buzzfeed,* September 6, 2017.

116 Diane Peterson, "'Silence Breaker' Lindsay Meyer Talks about Harassment in High-Tech," *The Press Democrat,* March 16, 2018.

117 Stephanie Zacharek, Eliana Dockterman and Haley Sweetland Edwards, "The Silence Breakers," *TIME,* December 6, 2017.

118 Diane Peterson, "'Silence Breaker' Lindsay Meyer Talks about Harassment in High-Tech," *The Press Democrat,* March 16, 2018.

world profoundly impacted him ... . In my most exhausted, worn-down, worn-out moment, I actually spent a portion of a flight crying and feeling some guilt, maybe some pain, maybe some sadness—it was really rooted in empathy for [the venture capitalist]. Which is just fucking twisted, right?"[119] It might be fucking twisted, but it's not uncommon.

By reporting, you unleash the potential to upend a life.

The scary part? The extent to which that life is upended isn't up to you. You can't control how the media, the public, and the system punish a person. It's what I realized the night frat-boy drunkenly screamed his fear at my friend. It's what Rachel avoided, by not reporting her locker-mate.

And that's the difference between sexual assault and other threats. If you want to protect a space, say that corner Tasty Burger or a small Jewish hometown or even an entire industry, the protocols are steadfast: you sense a risk, you call authorities. Others remain unharmed.

Take, for example, a strong rip current. When you report the rip current, you sprint from the ocean, having barely made it out, exhausted and soaking. You collapse in front of the lifeguard stand, panting about the danger, which is invisible until you're in it, but unavoidable once you are. There's no hesitation to protect your fellow swimmers because an undertow is just a natural force. No scholarship to take away, no schooling to suspend, no job or family to lose. It's easy to report when that report results in a red flag being raised by the beach, and people are simply told to stay out of the water for a bit.

When reporting comes with consequences beyond just a red flag, things aren't so simple.

---

119 Irin Carmon and Amelia Schonbek, "Was It Worth It?" *New York Magazine, The Cut,* September 30, 2019.

FAMILY MATTERS

———

*"We don't want to betray anyone—we don't want
to be the first to get curious and ask questions or
challenge the stories. We ask ourselves, How can I
love and protect my family if I'm rumbling with these
hard truths? For me, the answer to that question is
another question: How can I love and protect my
family if I'm not rumbling with these hard truths?"*

—BRENÉ BROWN

Switch.

I'm five years old. With a jagged front tooth and a scraggly
braid, I'm wearing a contraption that's some sort of cross
between glasses and goggles. The red, circular lenses cover
most of my face and slide in and out of wide plastic frames.
We're learning colors, starting with red.

Switch.

I drop blue lenses behind the red. The world changes—at
least, from where I'm looking. My younger sister, smiling up
at me, is now purple. Furiously curious, I reexamine everything in the room. What's our bunk bed like in purple? How

about our stuffed animal collection? And what about myself, in the mirror? We giggle, and she grabs the yellow set in her tiny palm, waving it up for me to try next. I slide out the red. *Switch.*

Kendall and I picked up on color mixing by the end of the afternoon, but new lenses kept sliding into place. On a burnt July evening the next year, our mom had a new baby. Left in the care of our grandpa, we put on matching yellow sundresses and hand-colored paper crowns that said "Welcome sister Daven," then went to the hospital to see her. We saw, and suddenly all of life looked different. Kendall traded her youngest-child lenses in: she was a big sister now too. And after that moment, I didn't see just one smile looking back up at me, but two.

Life unfolded from there, and lenses didn't stop shifting. The day I went to college; the afternoon my postgrad roommates and I moved into our sunny, first apartment; the bistro-lit night I met Dave. A new color slides into place on top of the old, and life looks the same but also indisputably different. A new shade to explore the world through.

Sexual assault, violence, rape—it's a lens-changer, too. If my world was purple, before, that night turned it indigo.

*

The front-porch-style life updates that buzzed between my mom, aunt, and grandmas never got less thorough. At ten years old, that worked in my favor. My bike and I were given complete freedom to roam our neighborhood, to hop from beach to beach, to explore the rocks and marshes and new friends' backyards. By virtue of the always-open line of communication between my mom and our family, she knew where I was. As a teenager, I appreciated that less.

At sixteen, I split a bottle of vodka with my friends after homecoming. When my parents found out, a couple weeks into November, it was not a small deal. Mom fumed, Dad laughed and then also fumed, and my entire family knew before I'd even processed how much trouble I was actually in. As the oldest child and oldest grandchild, there was no precedent for how to handle my infringement. A heavy disappointment grounded family gatherings for the next few months—I'm still not sure how much of it was my own. My behavior vibrated through generations, causing concern that wasn't there before. I squirmed under the weighted way my grandma looked at me, worried. *What was I up to?* That winter was especially cold. I never felt further from the front porch.

Switch.

When college started, my line of communication with the front-porch women was always open. I became a stream of life updates, big and small—any time I heard or did or learned something that demanded processing, someone in Niantic knew about it. Two weeks into freshman year, Mom and her mom visited. We traipsed across my city campus and had lunch at a fast-casual café. Nothing fancy. I just didn't feel like I could make a space my own until they'd seen it. Or I'd seen them in it.

The rest of that first year in Boston was marked by several two-hour trips to and from Niantic. I brought my roommate home for a baby shower. Kendall came up to spend the night in my twin XL. The summer after, I'd been home for a month, my grandma had a doctor's appointment in the city. Still in the rhythm of drives to and from Boston, I volunteered to go with her. Brit, Lina, and Mich were doing a summer semester up there, and their sunny frat party excursions sounded like a good time. After her appointment, my grandma drove home, and I spent the night with them.

Switch.

The next morning, I was on a Greyhound bus back to Niantic. The world was indigo.

I spent the bumpy ride exploring how everything looked in this new shade. The *Hope you're having fun!* text from Kendall, which once seemed simple, was suddenly poignant. The Tinder notifications, which were innocent enough yesterday, grossed me out through this new lens. What would friendships look like now that I knew how the world looked in indigo? Relationships? Family?

After that sixteen-year-old winter, I vowed to never risk isolation from my family again. I started drinking again the next year but asked my parents for permission before every party. I made a point of honesty with my grandparents too. No one looked at me like they were worried, and that weighted concern evaporated.

Except, now. It would be back. If I told them, it would be back. I couldn't risk that, and even though it would be born from a desire to protect me and/or to make some sense out of a senseless occurrence, I couldn't risk any one of my family members asking:

How much did you have to drink?

What were you wearing?

You consented to other stuff, though, right?

I wouldn't blame them. We're all doing the best we can. But the questions would make me want to seclude myself in a time when I needed connection more than anything.

I also imagined how, if I told them, they'd try to lift the sadness. They would try to carry it themselves, and as a result, feel these new, unpleasant, indigo feelings too.

My sisters were too young for this lens. My mom had two other daughters. She shouldn't have to see life through it either. And then—my dad.

I was fine. I would be fine. I'd figure out life in indigo, and just being in the same glowy beach town as my entire family would be helpful enough. I didn't need them to suffer too.

As the Greyhound pulled toward Niantic, I thought about other people I could tell. Maybe the police, maybe the university, maybe a lawyer. I wasn't sure. But I sensed that if I told any authority, the story might grow. And if I involved more characters, more people, more time, my family would feel it. There would be gaps in my constant communication. Unexplained details in the life updates. I existed in the arms of the women who raised me, and they'd feel my absence.

I still wonder if they felt any absence that summer, as I worked through it on my own.

Six years ago, I didn't report. Not even to my family. Three years later, I moved to California and had an idea for a book. *Unreported,* I'd call it, and it would be a collection of stories, including my own. But there was a snag—a fear that kept me from writing.

Why devote time and effort to a book that would make my family sad? Was it worth drafting? This book would turn people toward the truth and ask them to sit in its acidity. Was there value in that sorrow?

The shame and stigma of sexual violence is so real that, even with a front porch I felt sure would have me, I couldn't bring myself to report to my family.

Distance—six years, two cross-country moves, control over who knew my story and who didn't—has been healing. Like Dr. Christine Blasey Ford, who didn't tell her husband until years into their marriage, I wanted to wait to tell those who loved me most until my own pain subsided. Until I figured out what life looked like, in indigo. Now, I can show them.

ANAYA

Anaya is so much of everything. Intelligent, logical, decisive. When she makes a decision, it thunders. Like it's more of a natural force.

She decided to tell her parents. Unreported to authorities, informed with Mom and Dad. But her story is a lot more complex than that final, clear-headed decision.

Anaya's extended family was tight. The spend-a-month-together-every-summer sort of tight. Pile-three-families-into-a-three-bedroom-house sort of tight. Let-the-pack-of-cousins-stay-up-all-night-during-Ramadan sort of tight.

Forests are sometimes thinned to help prevent massively destructive fires. It seems to me that the logic goes something like this: the less dense the trees are, the harder it is for flames to catch. When trees are tight, brush growing over and around each other, branches intertwining, they can thrive. But they can also really burn.

Everyone in Anaya's family was close with one cousin in particular. Five years older than Anaya, he achieved star-child status. And, while all the cousins Skyped often during the eleven months they spent apart, Anaya talked with him the most.

"He was the person who I thought of as an older mentor, brother, kind of. Somebody I really trusted. And I really cared about his opinion. That type of thing," she says, as if it's just another fact.

The first time he laid hands on her inappropriately, and every time after that, she was confused. They were together for their annual family month in the summer. Fifteen years old, she would black out every couple days, becoming forgetful and nervous, faulting herself. She didn't know what to think. The one thing she did know? This could really burn.

The alive Ramadan nights and days spent sleeping, the cousins growing over and around each other—it all continued. It could have been magic, the type of moment you're nostalgic for before you even leave it.

"It's great," she says assuredly. "Unless you're doing that whole situation with someone who's assaulting you."

Anaya's the type of person who, even if you haven't talked in months, texts you a birthday message specific enough to show she's paying attention. She's lived all over the world and makes a point to call across time zones, carrying friends from each continent forward with her. She's loyal, protective, and eager. She'd stomp out a flame herself to protect the forest any day.

And that's exactly what she tried. Her family returned to the three-bedroom house for another celebratory month the next summer and, by then, she had stopped talking to her older cousin. Although he protested—"*Why are you ignoring me, Anaya?*"—she never started again.

Her silence was a statement.

He didn't touch her that summer. She didn't tell anyone, minus her best friend from Japan (who, in Anaya's words, "was pretty helpless, being a twenty-two-hour flight away").

"I was in my own head," she says, reflecting on that time period before any of her family knew. "It felt like a situation where, if you're going to tell someone, it's gonna be the end of the universe. Right? This is somebody who my whole family loves very much. My dad's older brother's son ... he was the best one, the one I was really good friends with too." She carried the secret through a second summer and into the school year.

Eventually, though, it started affecting her in ways she couldn't conceal.

Junior year, her grades plummeted. She failed all her classes; her parents thought she was just struggling to adjust. They hadn't moved back from Japan that long ago, after all.

She went on a date. And then another. On the third, the guy tried to kiss her. By traditional teen-movie standards, she was right on track. The plot hole, here? Traditional teen movies don't usually incorporate panic attacks.

Anaya's post-kiss panic attack raised a final, hyper-concerned red flag with her two best friends, Jane and Madison. It hadn't been her first—they'd both seen her experience several panic attacks already—and wouldn't be her last. After the third-date, first-kiss fiasco, Jane and Madison became the second and third to know Anaya's summer story.

"You can't keep seeing this person," they insisted, in shock that she'd returned for another family month even after her cousin had violated her the year before. And, as if the universe was testing their words, a physical invitation to see him arrived in the mail not long after.

Wedding invitations are intricate, ornate, timeless. They ask you to attend, but they also solicit something more. The bedazzled card stock itself is an invitation to imagine the ceremony—pure, intimate, safe—and the relationship—trusting, loving, good.

In the presence of her older cousin, those adjectives were absent. So, Anaya made up a million excuses not to attend the family wedding, where she knew he would be. When her parents left without her, she stayed at Madison's house.

The morning smelled like pancakes, so Anaya says she was suspicious before she even set foot into the kitchen. Madison's mom never made pancakes. The flapjacks were fluffy—Madison's mom was direct.

"Look, I know what's happening with you," Madison's mom began gently. "Your friends are really scared for you, and this is not sustainable or safe. When your parents come back today, I need you to tell them, or I will."

As a girl, when it comes to the topic of sex, moms can be easier to talk to first. As a girl about to broach the topic of sexual assault, they also can be easier to talk to first. When her parents got home from the wedding, Anaya began there.

"My one job," her mom sobbed. "How could I have messed up the most important thing?"

"It's not your fault," Anaya stopped her, strong.

"I felt horrible," she says, her voice thick, remembering years later.

Her mom offered to tell her dad, and moments later, he came up to her room. Knowing, devastated.

"I just want you to know," he assured her, "there is nothing in the world that could ever make me not care about you. No one else is ever more important. You are the only thing I care about in the situation, you have no reason to ever worry about me being mad at you, nothing could ever —"

"Anyway, it was really, it was really, really nice," she concludes.

And then life resumed. Anaya's family carried on. Her parents encouraged therapy, but she was given no responsibility beyond that. Her dad explained Anaya's older cousin's behavior to his brother, the boy's dad. His dad was furious, but not at his son. He refused to believe Anaya's story. The inevitable brushfire sparked.

Their father, Anaya's widowed grandpa, takes turns living with each of the families. "It's kind of a thing brown families do," she explains. Her dad drives cross-country to drop him off and pick him up. Now, it's the only interaction her father has with his brother.

"I'm glad my grandma never had to hear about this," Anaya sighs, in a thought that seems unrelated, but very much is.

A couple of years later, Anaya heard that the third family, her dad's younger sister and her daughters, were moving to the same town as her older cousin. The girls were younger than her, and the last summer they'd visited that three-bedroom house, one of them—Mira—wasn't talking to her much. Urgently, and as casually as she could muster, Anaya got them on Skype. In a florescent glow, under the guise of just talking about everything, Anaya made sure to talk about one thing.

When she finished telling her story, the one about why she stopped talking to her favorite older cousin, Mira blinked at her. *"You too?"* She half-asked, half-stated.

"I was crushed," Anaya remembers. "I wish I had done it earlier. I probably could have stopped some of what happened to her. I feel really bad about it. Always."

Anaya's family knows. Mira knows, in more ways than one. Madison and Jane know. But that's as far as she'll ever go.

"I thought about reporting at one point, but also, not really," she confides, before listing the many reasons it's not an option for her.

"There's no hard evidence, the statute of limitations is up. I mean, it took me over a year and a half to even tell anyone," she says. And when she did tell her mom, her first reaction was not to report either. *"What are we gonna do about it?"* she asked, taking responsibility herself, instead of reverting to law enforcement.

"And she thinks everyone should be in jail," Anaya adds, with a laugh.

In the past, when her dad's older brother and his family struggled, Anaya's family lent them money. "Gave," is the word she used, actually. Anaya calculates that, if legal fees were ever involved, it would be impossible to decipher which part of the family pot they were coming out of. Would her parents pay for her assailant's case?

"What the hell are we gonna be fighting?" she says. "Why would I battle my own family?"

Anaya thinks that, even if she had decided to report her own family member, her case wouldn't have made it very far. "The whole thing for me is that I wasn't even able to process anything until later. And that's not conducive to the legal system. I think any lawyers who I talked to about this, or a DA's office, even would have been like, 'Absolutely not. We have no understanding of what you're talking about happening.' Because even when you do talk about it, it's so vague, that it's not even ... I don't know what my case would look like."

Anaya's unreport saved her family money and further scorch. Six years later, free from the weight of more familial drama, she's healing.

Her parents are incredibly understanding, she says, crediting their sensitivity to her situation. Freshman year of college, her close friend was assaulted. "My parents are 100 percent there for those kinds of things. They understand things implicitly now in a way that I don't think they would have otherwise." She's closer with her grandpa, now. "He doesn't say much ... but when he hugs me now, you know, it's in a very different way. Things are better."

She majored in journalism at one of the top-ranked programs in the country. While still a student, she gravitated toward the sexual assault beat, and her talent was noticed not just by her school, but by an entire city. During her senior year, a story of hers was published in a national newspaper.

And Anaya went to therapy, as encouraged. After her first therapist implied that the assault probably happened because she's Muslim, she quickly found a new one. By the end of their first session, that second therapist diagnosed her with PTSD.

The PTSD and emotional upheaval are still a process—one that she's actively working through.

"It's definitely still bad, and I have a ton of anxiety and all these other things that are directly related [to the assault]," she says.

When considering the reporting process and involving law enforcement, she adds: "I wouldn't have been ready for that, not all. I don't know how it's possible that anyone is ready for that. Even two years later, I wouldn't have been ready for that. I can still barely talk about it for longer than ten minutes without having a whole—"

She cuts herself short. We'd been talking for an hour and thirteen minutes.

PHIL

In 2016, Morgan Freeman's voice boomed across the Dolby Theatre in Los Angeles.

"And the Oscar goes to …"

A curtain of sparkles and life-sized Oscar statues glistened behind him.

"Spotlight!" He grinned. The Dolby erupted.[120]

Long before the film grossed over forty-five million dollars and gown-clad producers thanked the *Boston Globe* journalists from the Dolby stage, those journalists huddled in their office, beginning what would become a

---

120 Oscars, "'Spotlight' Wins Best Picture," March 23, 2016, video, 03:12.

two-part article exposing the Catholic Church's history of covering up sex abuse by priests in and around Boston.[121] The story was big—they had the credible source it necessitated.

Their tip came from Phil Saviano. Or, perhaps more accurately, their box of tips. Phil was repeatedly sexually abused by his priest beginning in 1964, when he was just eleven years old.[122] It took decades, but eventually, Phil reported.

There's something inherently reflective about the holidays. Thousands of little white lights illuminate the season, and in their glow, life until that moment looks clear. Memories glisten, feeling more important and romantic than they did just weeks ago at Thanksgiving. Festive, familiar tunes play out, and nostalgia sets in to their sweet chime.

It was December of 1992, and Phil was forty years old. That holiday season, his mortality was more delicate than it ever had been—he'd been diagnosed with AIDS, and the outlook was grim. That holiday season, beneath the radiant warmth of Christmas lights, he went public with accusations against his priest for the first time.[123]

Not long after, others came forward with similar stories about the same man: "Safety in numbers—it's an old story, and in this issue, it really is true," he told *New York Magazine* recently.[124] But, initially, Phil was the only person who was able to go on record non-anonymously.

121 Michael Rezendes, "Church Allowed Abuse by Priest for Years," *The Boston Globe*, January 6, 2002.

122 Sarah Betancourt, "'Cardinal Law Allowed This to Happen': Abuse Survivors on Archbishop's Death," *The Guardian*, December 21, 2017.

123 Ibid.

124 Irin Carmon and Amelia Schonbek, "Was It Worth It?" *New York Magazine*, The Cut, September 30, 2019.

"I think the only reason [the church] agreed to forgo the NDA is because they figured I wasn't going to be around much longer to talk anyway," he said in an interview with *People.* Their assumption was fair—Phil's doctors had recently advised that he buy a burial plot.[125]

In 1993, after Phil sued the Catholic Diocese of Worcester, his abuser was sentenced to 275 years in prison.[126] A sense of justice prevailed for Phil, in more ways than one: a new medication was working for him, and his health improved drastically. Sensing that priest abuse was an issue affecting many in his area, Phil decided to use the years of life he'd been given back to create a community. By 1997, he established the New England chapter of Survivors Network of Those Abused by Priests (SNAP).[127] By 1998, he had a long list—too long—of pedophilic priests in Boston, and details about the high-level cover-ups that allowed them to stay in power. He went to the *Globe* then, but it wasn't until three years later in 2001 that they were willing to investigate the story at the level of depth it demanded.[128]

But this retelling is merely a timeline. There was a second story unfolding during those years: one that isn't as quantitative and hasn't been covered by the press, let alone Hollywood. One that you can't find many details on, even after pouring over the comprehensive list of media reports on PhilSaviano.

125 Mike Miller, "The Incredible Story of Spotlight's Phil Saviano: The Child Sex Abuse Survivor Who Refused to Be Silenced by the Catholic Church," *People,* February 5, 2016.

126 Sarah Betancourt, "'Cardinal Law Allowed This to Happen': Abuse Survivors on Archbishop's Death," *The Guardian,* December 21, 2017.

127 Mike Miller, "The Incredible Story of Spotlight's Phil Saviano: The Child Sex Abuse Survivor Who Refused to Be Silenced by the Catholic Church," *People,* February 5, 2016.

128 Sarah Betancourt, "'Cardinal Law Allowed This to Happen': Abuse Survivors on Archbishop's Death," *The Guardian,* December 21, 2017.

com. While Phil was building his own community at SNAP and rescuing the community of Boston via the press and the legal systems, he was also struggling to maintain his most core community. His family.

He told his brothers about the abuse first, sometime after it occurred and before the first newspaper article came out. Phil remembers the conversation in relation to another specific marker: it came just months after telling them he had AIDS.[129] Later, when his older brother ran into another person the priest had violated in town, they had a painful exchange.

"[The other person] said, 'we guys'—I guess other people he was talking to in my hometown—'couldn't understand why I was making such a big deal out of this,'" Phil recounted to *New York Magazine*. "And they kind of felt bad for [the priest]. He said, 'The only thing we could figure out is, Phil must be really angry he has AIDS, and he's taking it out on [the priest].'"[130]

It's tough to hear that story. But it might be especially tough, to hear that story from your brother. To feel his discomfort, his offense on your behalf. To watch as, in a single interaction, the abuse that isolated you for so long takes him captive too. To realize that he is also suffering, in a different way. His empathy cost him.

Phil waited longer to tell his dad. As long as he could, really.

"I didn't tell my father until the day before [*The Globe*] story came out ... he was at first sympathetic—he said just try not to think about it, put it behind you, get on with your life," Phil remembered.[131]

---

129 Irin Carmon and Amelia Schonbek, "Was It Worth It?" *New York Magazine, The Cut*, September 30, 2019.

130 Ibid.

131 Ibid.

When Phil clarified that he actually had told the *Globe* his story, his dad's tone changed. It intensified.

"He was no longer supportive, he was really angry with me," Phil said. "Because I was bringing a scandal to my hometown. Instead of thinking about myself, I should be thinking about him, and my poor aunt who had to live in that town and deal with the scandal and what it might say about the family. I finally said, 'You know what, Dad? When I was a kid, I didn't come to you because I kept thinking somehow I was going to get blamed for this.'"[132]

There was something in the room at the Dolby Theatre that night when Morgan Freeman announced "Spotlight!" and producers walked, gloriously, to the stage. Something that kept it full, buoyant, celebratory. It was support—universal and so real you could see it. Support got those producers through the grueling filmmaking process, through that night's never-ending ceremony, and onto that stage. Support got Phil through a traumatic court case and then ushered him into a new era of healing among peers as the SNAP New England founder. His brothers were supportive, journalists were supportive, and eventually, most of Boston supported him.

But the funny thing about support is just that. You can get it from so many places. You can settle a lawsuit, you can create an entire organization, you can have a celebrity depict you in an Academy-Award winning movie. But if you don't get support from where you need it most, you feel it. Even thick layers of other support can't patch that hole.

Eventually, the hole stopped aching. Phil's father filled it.

"My father finally came around, about a month into *The Globe*'s reporting ... he sent me a copy of the

---

132 Ibid.

church bulletin from my hometown. There was a message in the bulletin saying if anybody had been sexually assaulted as children, please come forward and come to the bishop and let us know. So, I called him up and I said, 'Geez, thanks. I'm surprised you sent this to me, but I'm glad you did.' And he said, 'Well, I've been reading all this stuff in the *Globe*, and I realize now that you've been right all along.'"[133]

When Phil speaks, each word echoes with emotion and a thick Boston accent. He has white hair and glasses and keeps one eyebrow raised, like he's always questioning something. For most of his life, maybe he was.

"He wouldn't believe his own son," Phil finished, speaking to *New York Magazine*, "but he believed the *Boston Globe*."[134]

His own son. The disbelief resonates there—the hurt feels evident in the way Phil makes his point. The way he takes ownership over his rank as it relates to his dad and emphasizes how that rank seemingly didn't matter. He needed support, but didn't get it until after the newspaper fanfare. Perhaps that hole was gaping too long.

It makes sense that a person wouldn't report to protect their family. To avoid watching them suffer, even just in their own empathy. Or to avoid suffering themselves, if that empathy doesn't come. It might feel safer to keep the assault from them, or, like Anaya did, tell them but keep it from authorities. She avoided monetary loss for her family and, in the absence of law enforcement, kept their severed ties private. Reporting didn't engorge familial flames because, beyond her parents, she chose to remain unreported.

---

133 Ibid.

134 Ibid.

Phil reported to the media—a viable, effective option to call for change as big as the one he needed. There's no question he was heroic and has embraced his role as an activist. But there's also no question the system, the only solution he had, deepened his pain before helping to heal it. The stigma of sexual violence meant he watched his brothers ache. It opened a hole his dad vacated instead of filling with support.

Switch.

In indigo, family can look different.

BIGGER OR SMALLER

———

"I understood that not everyone would welcome my information, and I was prepared for a variety of outcomes, including being dismissed."

—DR. CHRISTINE BLASEY FORD

The morning after is a complete blur.

I collect my clothes off the dorm room floor and hug concerned faces goodbye. If there is a conversation between Michelle, Lina, Brittany, and me, I later black it out. That happens sometimes, with trauma—I knew that even then. You black it out instead of letting it sink in.

What's the scale for trauma? I wonder, on my way to South Station. *Does that word fit what just happened to me?*

I board the Greyhound home and, as it revs, my mind moves more clearly. I slide deeper into the carpeted bus seat and plug my phone into the readily-available outlet—Mom cited this feature when she told me to take the bus home instead of the train. *It's okay, busses are so nice these days.*

Head pushed into the itchy seat fabric in front of me, I wonder if anyone else on the bus feels this heavy. Maybe there's another mind that just started navigating the same sort of dark maze of thought. Maybe they're on the other side of the headrest I'm pressed into, just as petrified, scared of the new story their brain had begun turning over.

I don't want to be having these thoughts. I didn't ask for the struggle of sorting them.

As the Greyhound screeches away from the night before, I know I can't ever let the thoughts stop. They're a twisted line in my story now. I'm not religious, but that morning, I pray. *Please don't let this line become my entire plot.*

The iPhone 5 doesn't make me dial all ten digits, thank god. My fingers are too exhausted for that. Two clicks and a ring in the receiver, and Elle picks up. She's been to parties at this frat before. She'll get it.

"Are you okay? Kale, what happened?"

"I'm gonna tell you something, and I just want you to tell me what you think, okay? I just don't know..."

And I whisper. Less to be polite, more because I am feverishly afraid that someone will hear what I'm saying. I'd never whispered quite like that before. But, I figure, maybe that's what people with real secrets (trauma?) do on busses.

The conversation lasts eleven minutes and thirty-seven seconds. Eleven minutes and thirty-seven seconds, and only three words sink in.

"Yes, that's rape."

I can't see Elle's eyes as I stumble through my story, but her words tell me enough. Yes, the news is acidic.

The Greyhound lands me back in that calm coastal town. The place that sheltered me and protected me, for better or for worse, until now. I climb salt-caked rocks and collapse in front of a gray ocean with two hometown friends and one new secret. Smiling feels wrong but eventually, to avoid alarming them, I find one. My eyes don't match. They don't notice.

Summer spins on.

I stuff myself into business attire and go spend a day at Naomi's software start-up. It strikes a new nerve, when the older male employees lower their voices and slip in comments about how I am a beautiful young lady. Over and over during those first few post-freshman year months, I am profoundly disappointed by men in the real world.

So, I take a break from that world.

I get a job at a boutique in town and give myself one last summer by the bay. My partner-in-crime, MK, is thrilled. She lives in a summer cottage up the street from June through August, and we've spent the last nine summers together.

She's the second person I tell, over raw cookie dough and ice cream on her parents' front porch. She tears up, holds my hand, and agrees to help me escape my new real-world secret by swinging into lakes and dancing with bonfire flames. Almost magically, it starts to fall away, behind bike rides and skinny dips and hot, sandy afternoons. Every time she makes me laugh, I feel further from that night. I find smiles faster—my eyes start to go with them.

And then I find a summer fling. Liam. He hangs with the same people as MK and I, and I had hidden a crush on him for years. We camp on the beach and steal a tent for ourselves. We trek to house parties and leave early to look at stars from the field next door. We kiss for the first time, and for the first time in my life I feel fragile. We kiss again, and every time I pull away it feels different. Like I'm pulling away protectively. Liam's the third person to know. We're nineteen and twenty and our friends are hooking up at house parties and in tents on the beach. We don't.

I was nervous to tell Liam. When I did, his reaction wasn't what I expected. His eyes turned down as he listened to the story, but there was something beyond concern in them. It felt like admiration. Respect, maybe. He hugged me, and when he let go, I felt strong.

After that, telling men becomes a part of being with them. I gauge their secondary reactions, evaluate the words they respond with, and factor that into my feelings for them. It's impossible not to. In that secondary reaction, you learn about the person listening.

That nineteen-year-old summer goes down as a period of extreme healing. Surrounded by MK and our pure fun and Liam and his simple affection, the return to health is almost expedited. A year later, July comes again, and I am in love for the first time since the secret/trauma/assault/rape occurred. Arthur is good with words and exemplifies my dream response (or so I thought; how can you ever really know what your dream response is to telling someone you were assaulted?).

"*I'll beat him up,*" he huffs, in an octave lower than his speaking tone. "*You never should have had to go through that. I'm so sorry.*" We're sitting on a dock in the small beach town that raised us both, safe, dipping our toes in the bay. I lean into his side, and I stay. My eyes tear up, but I think it's gratitude that's filling them.

"*No one should.*" I wonder if I sound as sure as I feel, in that moment.

After college, I move West and many things change. Litmus testing potential boyfriends doesn't. I keep finding new reactions: while Liam projected strength onto me and Arthur summoned strength himself, other men surprise me. One quietly responds, "*Me too.*" He'd been assaulted by an older man. Another shifts in his seat during a road trip up the California coast, recounting a night in college where he'd been assaulted by a woman.

And then there's the prospect who responded with a, *"Well ... you were drunk, right?"* I'd finished talking, but in the wake of that reaction it felt like he cut my story short.

Well ... he countered. Playing devil's advocate. No need to advocate for Satan, in the moments after someone vulnerably tells you how she was violated.

You. Not his fault. Yours.

Right? As if "right" would tie the bow on his argument, sealing the subject. He wasn't factually incorrect. I was drunk. Not too drunk to say no. Not too drunk to say it again and again and again. But even if I had been, does that excuse the frat boy's actions?

Wrong.

It was the wrong secondary reaction, the wrong words, and it was suddenly obvious that he was the wrong person. We'd been friends for a year and dating for a month, so when he started with, "Well ..." my throat tightened. I didn't want to hear it from him. I didn't want his words to cement my fear that he didn't believe me, or didn't care.

Or my deeper fear, that I wasn't worthy of belief. That the situation didn't demand care.

The romantic prospect minimized the night, my pain, the process of healing I was in. While it was hard to hear his reaction, it was easy to navigate my next step. I minimized his role in my life and decisively kept moving forward, without him.

I used to say that I couldn't imagine having an authority minimize my pain with a statement like that. How much you had to drink would be a standard, even necessary, question during the reporting process. I couldn't imagine a cop asking and raising his eyebrows as he recorded the answer.

But then, I guess I can. I did imagine it, which is part of why I didn't report. No one was allowed to minimize my pain, including and especially not men. I made sure of it.

What I truly can't imagine—don't want to imagine—is not being free to dismiss someone who does. To hear or watch or feel a judge or jury of any kind minimize the assault, and then be unable to move forward without them. I had the authority to let go of that romantic prospect without checking with anyone, and that was empowering. We were in no way tied, and so when he made me uncomfortable, I called the shots and left him.

It felt like taking back a piece of that night years earlier. That night when I thought I was calling the shots, but was trapped.

I had no interest in going to the police, and become trapped again; this time, inside legality and paperwork and investigation. In fact, I was scared of it. I needed to navigate healing on my own, with the power to walk away from a situation the moment I felt uncomfortable.

When I was stuck that night, I pushed the frat boy down and propelled myself out. When I was uncomfortable with the romantic prospect years later, I simply turned around and walked away. But I couldn't escape like that from law enforcement. If they didn't believe me, or didn't care, I couldn't kick them to the floor, pants around their legs. I couldn't text them later, explaining that unfortunately I didn't really want to see them anymore. I would be immobilized by their minimization, unable to move forward.

With nowhere to go, I was afraid I'd internalize it.

GRACIE

Gracie is a type. For anyone who's watched a rom com set in a small town, she's *the* type. The fiercely-intelligent-but-interested-in-so-much-more-than-books type. She grew up while wandering around town, twirling a strand of long, red hair in her fingers, staring at the sun, and wondering how she could make the lives of her neighbors better.

Girls love her for her wild imagination. A Sunday plan with Gracie goes beyond just brunch. Instead, she does things she enjoys. Things no one else remembers that they enjoy too: bracelet-making, water coloring, driving until you finally find that swimming hole you heard about that one time. She's a human reminder that life is here to be lived deeply, and she giggles at any and every joke that comes her way. Sometimes, it feels like she's giggling at life.

Boys love her for all those reasons, too. Plus, she has a tiny waist, wide-set hips, and an affinity to ultra-feminine sundresses that flounce when she walks.

She's the type. And when she went to college, she became a prototype. You might see a little of yourself, in Gracie.

Before, she didn't think it was going to happen to her. But years later, she says she's had a realization: "It's so common and disgusting."

Reflecting on the moment it did happen to her, she adds, "I lost all trust in the male race, in the wee hours of that night."

The thing about trust is, it's an unstandardized measurement. Some people take years to trust one another, to really count them as a friend. Before that night, Gracie was on the other end of the spectrum. She threw trust around; not haphazardly, but in a way that reflected her optimistic outlook. It's part of what made her so easy to be around.

Take that night, for example. She trusted her friends, and her friends trusted this guy. Therefore, by the principles of any optimist's generous faith, Gracie trusted the friend-of-a-friend. Surrounded by sloshy beer, a crowd of people packed in her dorm room, and a new friend, she was on the precipice of becoming the prototype for college rape.

Whether or not friend-of-a-friend deserved the trust she gave him is a different story. This story revolves around the fact that he broke it. They were both drunk, but not too drunk to say no. Not too drunk to be decent human beings.

Where is that limit? When is a person drunk enough to excuse being a bad human being? Why do we speak as if it exists?

It was three o'clock in the morning when he left her dorm, looking guilty.

"Immediately after, I opened my dorm door and the only other door that was open were these two girls down the hall that I barely knew," Gracie remembers. "They were a year older than me, and I sort of explained what happened. They felt bad but they kind of 'sloughed' it off and didn't really offer help."

She retreated to her room and faced her bed, the twin XL. She stared at it for a beat, and then made a decision. "I went to sleep at a friend's house that night because I was so grossed out to sleep in my own bed where it happened," she explains.

While at her friend's, Gracie didn't sleep soundly. "Right after it happened that night ... was the most terrifying few hours of it all, honestly. I was like, wow, I'm in trouble, I need to tell people. But then after I slept, I felt so different about it all. My logic took over my emotion, and made me not file a report."

And so began Gracie's journey. The hero's journey, for college girls. Prototypical and, sometimes, profound. But never singular.

Before Gracie had time to process her own pain, her friends were questioning her about it over omelets and hangovers at breakfast the next morning. *"Yeah, but it was a party, you had fun,"* pressed her roommate, who had been the mastermind behind the gathering.

"Most people just said 'move on' ... they didn't take it very seriously," Gracie reflects, lost back in that morning-after memory. Then she adds, "It's not that they didn't care, but they were kind of like, 'It happens to everyone, so just deal with it.'"

Just deal with it.

Just accept that your "no" meant nothing to this friend-of-a-friend. Just deal with the fact that, when you are violated, you are subjected to a completely individual pain and yet, you simply become one of many. Just tolerate that the system is not built to protect you.

You might argue that she could have protected herself. That she should have been careful about how much she had to drink, what she was wearing, or could have held the party in a place other than her 8'x8' dorm room, where two beds occupied most of the space. An older and wiser woman might insist that Gracie was too naive anyway, and that her innocence had to go, someday.

It's part of growing up.

To that, I say this: there are other ways to lose your innocence. Ways you can choose. You can become a fully responsible, mature woman, without experiencing sexual violence. We should all be given that grace. The real question is, how many of us actually are?

So, Gracie became a prototype, and as her friends minimized the assault, she was pushed further into the role. It's a signature feature of this college-girl model, to believe that what happened to them wasn't "serious enough."

"I'm lucky in a sense that I was able to recover without any mental or physical health consequences," she told me. "In the grand scheme of things, it's bad but it's not the worst thing that could've happened to me. I wasn't injured or anything like that."

And Gracie's right. She wasn't left behind a dumpster. She wasn't fourteen. It wasn't her cousin. Her knowledge of other stories helps her minimize her own. It helps all of us. But the thing is, there will always be a worse situation. Comparing pain helps you feel less unlucky, but it doesn't help you heal. It doesn't help you connect with others, who are also healing.

Gracie's friends minimized her pain, and eventually Gracie did too.

"I didn't report because I felt like I could have done more to prevent it from happening in the first place," she admits. "Although he was on top of me, I could have pushed him off or fought him, clawed at him, or any form of self-defense. It's weird though because you're just paralyzed—with fear, sadness, shock. I didn't even try to move. I think because of that I didn't want to report because they would have asked 'did you physically try to stop him?' and I would have had to say no. And I would feel stupid for even reporting it or considering it rape in the first place."

This is Gracie anticipating the questions, the doubt, the minimization. She experienced it from her friends, without much of a choice. They minimized her pain over breakfast— not because they were cruel, but because they were conditioned by society to treat it casually. And, probably, somewhat scared. After that, her hurt wasn't even allowed to fully exist inside her own mind. She couldn't think about it without a chorus of "but you could have" objections butting in, drowning out whatever the pain was trying to tell her.

Can you blame her, for not wanting to give a person of authority the power to reinforce that minimization?

When her friends minimized the situation, it was uncomfortable. When she minimized it to herself, it was confusing. Imagine a uniformed officer downplaying the night's events, even in the slightest. Imagine how hard it would be, to feel that authority imply that she could have done more or trusted less.

"It's weird because when it happens, you're in such shock from the event that you don't want to immediately talk to authorities. So, then you sleep on it, and in the morning, you wake up feeling like it was almost a dream?" she says, trailing the end of her sentence up into a question. "Like did that really happen? And then you start to think, okay, is it worth telling? Does my story sound stupid? Do I have enough evidence? And then you convince yourself to just get on with your life and try to forget about it."

What happened to Gracie was minimized in many places, but nowhere with finality. There aren't any legal documents signed, sealed, and delivered that decide, officially, that the assault wasn't "serious enough." Instead of risking that outcome, Gracie did exactly what she intended to, after her unreport.

She continued living.

Five years older and wiser, Gracie works full time and has a supportive, mature partner who inspires her to be her best. After college, she moved to a new place where she fell in love with the community, the people, and the control she has over her situation.

Gracie still wonders what exactly happened to her that night. Was it assault, rape, or "just something that happens to everyone"? She wonders, but she does not debate it. Without any authorities to tell her otherwise, the memory is free to feel as big or small as it wants to be, on any given day. When she sees her assailant on social media, it swells. In other moments, she's able to "just bury it like a common burden of life." But, since the assault was not formally minimized, she can process it at her own pace. The size and significance remain firmly and solely in her control.

LINDA

When he assaulted her, twenty years ago, he was a household name.

Linda Vester was one of the youngest correspondents at the network back in those days, and every bit the up-and-comer. Motivated, savvy, striving. A good relationship with a well-established superior, an anchor known and loved by Americans across the country, could help expedite her success. At the very least, a connection like that could help up her clout around the office. But before long, the promising relationship morphed. The established anchor assaulted her. She went unreported.[135]

For twenty years, Linda managed the pain and healing process on her own. For twenty years, no one could minimize it.

But then, in the throes of the #MeToo movement, a different famous NBC host was facing sexual assault allegations from too many women.[136] One is too many, if you've experienced it, but, as we've seen, one can be brushed off. This

---

135 Elizabeth Wagmeister and Ramin Setoodeh, "Tom Brokaw Accused of Sexual Harassment by Former NBC Anchor (Exclusive Video)," *Variety,* April 26, 2018.

136 Ramin Setoodeh and Elizabeth Wagmeister, "Matt Lauer Accused of Sexual Harassment by Multiple Women (Exclusive)," *Variety,* November 29, 2017.

number of accusations was more difficult to downplay. The story broke early in the morning. As news stations nationwide wrapped up their initial coverage, one of the many women who publicly accused the host called Linda.[137]

"We were both quaking with an anxiety we couldn't name," Linda remembered, in an interview with *The Cut*.[138] But for Linda, that unnamed anxiety spouted from a different source than it did for the woman who called her. The famous NBC host in headlines that morning had assaulted the woman on the other end of the line, but not Linda. No one had named Linda's assailant—yet.

Perhaps Linda was quaking with anxiety about the sheer similarity of their stories. It must have been jarring to realize that the pain she'd carried for years was shared by so many others. And it must have been infuriating to realize that her assailant wasn't the only famous man who had used his flourishing career to prey on women. Perhaps she was shaking because her experience twenty years earlier was less unique than she'd realized, in her unreported isolation.

Or maybe the anxiety came from the knowledge of what she was about to do next.

When Linda was assaulted decades before, there were risks attached to reporting. Her experience could have been minimized, her career could have been hurt, her image tarnished. But #MeToo was a game changer. Right? The movement had the power to sweep people into a web of relative safety when they reported. A web that hadn't existed before.

---

137 Irin Carmon and Amelia Schonbek, "Was It Worth It?" *New York Magazine, The Cut*, September 30, 2019.

138 Ibid.

Linda put her faith in the apparent progress of society. She went public with her story about the established anchor, granting an interview to the *Washington Post* and recording a video for *Variety*.[139] [140] In the latter, she sits upright on a couch against a plain wall. Wearing all black—maybe in mourning of sorts—she articulates exactly and emphatically how her superior crossed the line multiple times with her.

The story begins with the established anchor coming to her hotel room one night while they were both shooting onsite, and ends with her on the couch, holding a throw pillow like a shield. *"I guess I should go,"* the established anchor said, before leaving. The next year, a similar incident occurred.[141]

When Linda reported her allegations to the press, there was no standard #MeToo cancellation of the established anchor. Instead, in a 4:00 a.m. email to a smattering of other high-profile media figures, he told the story his way. He admitted to "a perfunctory goodnight kiss," and said, in that belittling certainty that sometimes seems reserved for men, that Linda always had a hard time with truth.[142]

"What was her goal?" he asked. "Hard to believe it wasn't much more Look at Me than Me Too."[143]

---

139 Elizabeth Wagmeister and Ramin Setoodeh, "Tom Brokaw Accused of Sexual Harassment by Former NBC Anchor (Exclusive Video)," *Variety,* April 26, 2018.

140 Sarah Ellison, "NBC News Faces Skepticism in Remedying in-House Sexual Harassment," *The Washington Post,* April 26, 2018.

141 E Elizabeth Wagmeister and Ramin Setoodeh, "Tom Brokaw Accused of Sexual Harassment by Former NBC Anchor (Exclusive Video)," *Variety,* April 26, 2018.

142 Lisa de Moraes, "Tom Brokaw Blasts Ex-colleague 'Who Had Trouble with the Truth' and News Outlets That 'Perp Walked' Him," *Deadline,* April 27, 2018.

143 Ibid.

The established anchor's denial didn't surprise Linda, but she was surprised at how mean and personal he was in his attack of her character. "His vehemence and spitefulness took me aback," she said.[144]

Even that shock, though, couldn't have prepared Linda for what came next.

A long list of women at NBC, including several famous female TV personalities, signed a letter in support of the anchor.[145] While it's possible to hypothesize about how anxious Linda might have felt in the moments before she went public with her accusations—reporting to the media is, after all, still reporting—I find it nearly impossible to imagine how she must have felt, with the signatures of her colleagues staring back at her.

"[The anchor] has treated each of us with fairness and respect," they wrote. "He has given each of us opportunities for advancement and championed our successes throughout our careers. As we have advanced across industries—news, publishing, law, business and government—[he] has been a valued source of counsel and support. We know him to be a man of tremendous decency and integrity."[146]

The letter makes no mention of Linda by name. But, as it was published in the wake of her claims, it's difficult to separate its existence from her accusations. *He's a good guy*, the letter alleges. Which, as Linda explained in an editorial for the *Washington Post*, is unrelated.

"I came forward for a simple reason," she wrote. "To let the public know that otherwise good men—men who treat

---

144 Irin Carmon and Amelia Schonbek, "Was It Worth It?" *New York Magazine, The Cut,* September 30, 2019.

145 Ibid.

146 Katie Kilkenny, "Rachel Maddow, Andrea Mitchell Back Tom Brokaw in Letter Signed by 64 Insiders," *The Hollywood Reporter,* April 27, 2018.

women well or are even their champions—can also commit acts of sexual harassment. I did not feel like confronting [the anchor] in private would accomplish my objective of demonstrating to other victims—past, present or future—that it is safe to come forward with their own accounts of harassment in the workplace."[147]

Was it safe, though?

If safety is defined as "the condition of being protected from or unlikely to cause danger, risk, or injury," was it safe for Linda to come forward with her account?[148] Did her reputation emerge without injury? Was her integrity not put at risk? The anchor still works at NBC news, despite a second woman having accused him of sexual assault as well. He's still a household name.

In the past year, former employees at NBC News have been questioned by the New York attorney general's office about how the company handled sexual harassment allegations in the division—Linda was one of them. The attorney general's office doesn't comment on cases, and no one involved is able to say much.[149] Justice might be unfolding, but that unfold is slow.

And, in the meantime, that semi-under-wraps investigation of NBC News is not what shows up when you Google Linda. Instead, it's headlines about her accusation, with a new title attached as a wordy appendage to her name: *[Famous-anchor]-accuser Linda Vester.*

---

147 Linda Vester, "Why I Revealed That Tom Brokaw Harassed Me," *The Washington Post,* May 9, 2018.

148 Merriam-Webster Online, "safety," accessed February 19, 2021.

149 Stephen Battaglio, "New York Attorney General's Office Questioned NBC News Employees on Sexual Harassment," *Los Angeles Times,* May 5, 2020.

There was no quick trial in Linda's case. No decision by the court of public opinion to disavow the beloved TV personality who assaulted her. Instead, we are left with questions. Heaps of unanswered, and often, unasked questions. Most pressingly: what was it about her story that made people less inclined to care? Was it that he never penetrated her, or even succeeded in laying his lips on her? What didn't resonate in her report? And, whatever it was:

Is it fair that the lack of a deeper pain minimizes the existence of the pain she did feel?

The established, senior anchor came to her apartment unwanted. For a much-younger woman, who holds significantly less power professionally and physically, that can be frightening. Linda felt uncomfortable and violated. Yet, there was no acknowledgment of that when her colleagues signed a letter in support of her assailant.

Linda finally went through with the report that she did not make twenty years earlier. In the time since, she has not seen justice. Just a list of names supporting her assailant, and an email he wrote minimizing their interactions.

IN PURSUIT OF A FAIR OUTCOME

———

"I got my own back."

—MAYA ANGELOU

In high school, math became a maze. Solving for x and writing proofs felt like fun; maybe it was the figuring-it-out and providing evidence part that got me. But then, terms like *tessellation* came to the table, and my brain refused to compute. *Convergence, helix, multivariate*—I seemed to lack the capacity to wrap my head around any of these words. The first of the worst? Compound fractions.

Fractions were frustrating enough, and then they existed with other numbers. And then they were impossible.

*

Emma would not let it go.

As 2013 ended and 2014 began, I rounded out semester one in Boston. A giggly member of way too many group chats, the blue hue of my phone kept me tethered to new friends—people I was destined to love forever, I was sure. We Snapchatted and fired memes and posted birthday collages that were both elaborate and embarrassing (but by no means were we embarrassed by how elaborate they were). I instinctively smiled whenever one of their names buzzed into my notifications.

Between notifications, I scrolled—practically an automatic body function for a nineteen-year-old. After a particularly inspirational documentary film professor advised us to take in news both regularly and critically, my scrolling was often through news apps. It was years before Dr. Christine Blasey Ford took the stand, a year before Chanel was found behind a dumpster, and months before I was chased out of a frat house. But, as my thumb moved up and down the screen, it was impossible not to see a pattern in the headlines:

"100,000 Assaults. 1,000 Rapists Sentenced. Shockingly Low Conviction Rates Revealed"[150]

"Alabama Man Won't Serve Prison Time for Raping 14-Year-Old"[151]

"Montana Rapist Freed after Month-Long Sentence"[152]

And, maybe most hauntingly, *"Prosecuting Sexual Assault: Raped All over Again"*—a piece on Frances Andrade, a person who had been raped who killed herself days after she was cross-examined in court.[153]

---

150 Nigel Morris, "100,000 Assaults. 1,000 Rapists Sentenced. Shockingly Low Conviction Rates Revealed," *The Independent*, January 10, 2013.

151 Molly Redden, "Alabama Man Won't Serve Prison Time for Raping 14-Year-Old," *Mother Jones*, November 15, 2013.

152 Kyung Lah, "Montana Rapist Freed after Month-Long Sentence," *CNN*, September 26, 2013.

153 Amelia Gentleman, "Prosecuting Sexual Assault: 'Raped All over Again,'" *The Guardian*, April 13, 2013.

Snow mounds on either side, I read that headline on a particularly blustery walk to class one day and got chills.

Boston's frigid season was bad, but this news pattern? It felt like I was slipping around on black ice, each story reinforcing the existence of some dangerous unseen. Hood up and head down, I developed a growing, ominous suspicion: the world does not look out for women the way women look out for each other. Nationwide, according to my news apps, women were being violated, discarded, and denied justice. This was a much colder reality than the one I'd grown up in, on warm and genuine front-porch evenings with my mom, aunt, and grandmothers. The juxtaposition made me nervous, but having not yet fallen through the ice, it mostly fascinated me.

And then there was Emma. Emma Sulkowicz, a student at an Ivy League college. Emma, who quickly became my favorite developing news story. Emma, who would not let it go.

She filed a rape complaint with her school in 2013, explaining that she was compelled to report after meeting two other students who had similar accusations against her assailant.[154] I could almost hear the exchange—between women, they're that common. The first person would have mentioned his name in some mild, unrelated context: *One of my classes is so small, it's just me, this girl, and [the assailant]*—and she'd pause for a beat when she noticed how the person she was talking to tightened. *He's so creepy,* the second person would say, as if that could be the end of it. But it wouldn't be because as it would turn out, that subtle statement was just the beginning of what they had in common. This is how women find patterns before anything hits headlines. No collusion, just conversation.

---

154 Amanda Taub, "Columbia's Response to Campus Rape Is "Prolonged, Degrading, and Ultimately Fruitless," *Vox*, October 3, 2014.

Emma was looking out for all three of them, and by extent all her other female classmates, when she took official action. But the college did not return the favor. They found him "not responsible," and I remember wondering what the threshold was, there.[155] If three wasn't enough, how many accusations would have been? Was there any world in which the verdict might have tilted the other way?

After eight months of inaction, the women gave interviews to the *New York Post*.[156] I followed their logic: the local college system hadn't protected them, so maybe the press could. Headlines came and went, and Emma appeared with Senator Kirsten Gillibrand at a press conference about campus sexual assault. The thrice-accused assailant continued his college career, unpunished.[157]

What was the college waiting for? I wondered.

Then, as the East Coast thawed, twenty-three students took it to the federal level. They filed a complaint against their college for violating Title IX of the Education Amendments of 1972: their list of grievances included failure to remove perpetrators from campus, lenient sanctions, and discouraging students from ever reporting in the first place.[158]

As I packed up my freshman dorm, the fascinated fear intensified: twenty-three seemed like a high number. Could the university really ignore that many women?

---

155 Tara Palmeri, "Columbia Drops Ball on Jock 'Rapist' Probe: Students," *New York Post*, December 11, 2013.

156 Ibid.

157 CBS NY, "Sen. Kirsten Gillibrand Seeks Funds to Fight College Campus Sex Assaults," *CBSN NY*, April 2, 2014.

158 Emma Bogler, "Students File Federal Complaint against Columbia, Alleging Title IX, Title II, Clery Act Violations," *Columbia Spectator*, April 24, 2014.

I realized that it could. In ignoring any, it already had.

Whatever sexual assault reporting system the university had in place, it failed Emma. Reporting to the press failed her as well. A federal complaint could not affect the immediate change she wanted. The change she needed, which was relatively simple: to stop running into her assailant on campus. So, on May 14, 2014, Emma filed a complaint with the NYPD.[159] I was watching her case closely now, and I was optimistic.

The police would do it. Finally.

And then a month later, I was running toward a Lyft, being chased by an angry, stumbling man. Scared and confused, with friends around me, newly alone. As we drove across the Charles River, talking about how *weird* the night was, I thought about Emma. What she had learned, and what I had inferred.

She reported to every system she could, and still didn't have a fair outcome.

For most of the year, Boston is a gray city: cement pushed up against overcast skies, decked almost solely by faded American Revolution–era statues. I walked the Freedom Trail and circled the Common, and, despite knowing I was supposed to feel otherwise, remained flatly uninspired by men on horses with swords. During my time there, I instead came to love a largely overlooked Beantown staple: The Hyatt Regency. A hotel across the Charles, it became my favorite view—an honorary monument. It's massive and interesting and from the Esplanade you can't miss it. Someone built it to look like steps, and I was captivated by the way they led right into the sky. During night walks, I'd quietly worship the way it

---

159 Emma Bogler, "Frustrated by Columbia's Inaction, Student Reports Sexual Assault to Police," *Columbia Spectator*, December 28, 2016.

sparkles, faithfully lighting up the river it reflects into like a sort of promise.

That transformative night, after escaping, we sped down Storrow Drive and the Hyatt caught me like it always had before. As its lights blurred, my thoughts shifted to numbers. An unlikely place, as I'd given them up years before. But things were adding up now: the way Naomi's face had fallen during our meeting weeks before. The fact that Emma was still waiting to hear back from the police. The hundreds of headlines that hadn't ever stopped. My experience moments before. Each story was a fraction of the truth: the world does not look out for women. Not the way women do for each other. For the first time that night, the stair-shaped Hyatt looked like steps to nowhere.

Taken together, our stories felt like a compound fraction. Impossible.

I spent that summer entirely wrapped up in my new reality, grappling with how to heal and only slightly conscious of the fact that I chose not to report. In August, my phone alerted me: NYPD cited "lack of reasonable suspicion" against Emma's assailant. They weren't pressing charges.[160] The police failed her too.

I'd seen her face before, but now Emma looked like me. Not literally: she was two years older, starting her senior year in New York while I kicked off sophomore year in Boston. She was Asian and had edgy, purple-streaked hair. My blonde strands were always back in a bun that was almost undone. But after that summer, I recognized myself in her eyes.

As we returned to our own campuses, each with her own new sad summer story to bear, Emma returned to my news

160 Christopher Robbins, "Spurned by Columbia, Student Says NYPD Mistreated Her While Reporting Rape," *Gothamist,* May 18, 2014.

alerts. That September, she existed on all my feeds: her picture plastered to the top of articles that were shared again and again. But it wasn't a verdict that was going viral. It was her art.

For Emma's senior thesis, she created a striking piece of performance art: *Mattress Performance (Carry That Weight)*. She carried a 50-lb mattress around with her all year—the same size as the twin-XL on which she'd been attacked. She announced, defiantly, that she'd continue carrying it until her assailant stopped going to school with her. Did she know, by that point, that she'd carry it across the stage with her at graduation?[161]

All year, Emma and her mattress were shared on my timeline. She never let it go. My network applauded it as genius performance art, and I liked each of their posts (pressing "like" loaded with a little too much feeling). I supported her, I supported the increasingly widespread dialogue about campus sexual assault, and I wondered if maybe art could finally create the change she had sought for so long. I also wondered about the people posting the pictures of Emma and her twin-XL, though. Were their shares indicative of something? When I meekly reposted the link, without a caption, it definitely was. Before I was ready to tell my entire virtual sphere, Emma's art did some of the talking for me.

She spent years reporting to different systems and found no justice there. So, she turned elsewhere. Made her own justice, alone with her art.

"To me, the piece has very much represented [the fact that] a guy did a horrible thing to me and I tried to make something

---

161 Roberta Smith, "In a Mattress, a Lever for Art and Political Protest," *The New York Times*, September 21, 2014.

beautiful out of it," she said.[162] When I scrolled through her interviews, now, I was fascinated for different reasons.

Without a functional justice system to solve for sexual violence, this is what we do, I realized, as I packed up my sophomore year and Emma finished her senior spring with a mattress on her back. *We figure out how to make our own fair outcomes.*

By the time I watched Emma walk across the graduation stage, mattress and media coverage in tow, I knew this was her justice. Or at least, as close as she could come to it, without any system to create it for her. As she flipped her tassel, I remember feeling grateful that I wouldn't spent two years of college wrapped up in those systems. I wouldn't alternate reports through each of them, becoming more dejected, with no justice to speak of. I'd remain unreported.

But, like Emma, I couldn't let it go. What was a fair ending for my story?

*

Compound fractions aren't actually impossible. You can work with them easily, if you convert them into simple fractions first.

It's a numbers game. I knew that. One in five.[163] I didn't like math, but that statistic helped move me away from self-doubt and blame—*What was it about me? What could I have done differently?*—and into the straightforward acceptance that, because of probability, I simply had a chance.

162 Andy Battaglia, "Will Emma Sulkowicz's Protest Mattress Wind up in a Museum?" *Vulture,* May 28, 2015.

163 "Statistics," RAINN (Rape, Abuse & Incest National Network), accessed March 5, 2021.

But it's a wicked numbers game. Because after it happens once, you aren't taken out of the equation. You return to the general pool again—just another woman with a 20 percent chance of being picked.

Four years later, another fraction. An infraction. I'd never said anything to my freshman year assailant. I was still processing what a fair ending might look like for that story—some vague ideas about a book, maybe? But four years later, when it happened again, I knew. It would be more immediate. I could work with the compound fraction by simplifying.

He left his watch. I think intentionally. As if we might see each other again. As if he hadn't—

It was a crappy watch, but I made a big deal out of dropping it off for him. He texted back, seeing an opportunity. *Maybe we could also grab a—*

No, I'm in a rush. Sorry. Can you actually just come to my car?

The car window was already down (it was California, it was always down). I handed the cheap piece of silver out to him without a smile. The awkwardness was palpable. My heart was racing. Watch returned, I thought about how much time had changed me as I pulled away.

Fewer than sixty seconds after the hand off, I turned a corner, pulled over, and copied and pasted a text from my notes app. It took me a while to draft that morning, but I wanted it to hit him immediately that afternoon, while he was still quaking from our interaction, hopefully wondering why it had been so weird.

"I want you to know that I'm not really comfortable," the text began. "Please be more considerate of consent with people in the future," it ended. In between, the words weren't unkind, but forceful enough to make an impression.

It wasn't justice, but it was as close as I would come, without any system to create it.

ELIZAH

Fractions aren't the only things that compound. Trauma does too.

Trouble sleeping. Flashbacks from the assault showing up in nightmares. Anxiety-dominated decision-making. Mistaking safety and danger. A hug from a partner feeling "unsafe" one moment and the absence of his arms inducing panic the next. That's what compound trauma looked like, to Elizah.

"I would say two years ago, I started having PTSD symptoms," Elizah said, her voice almost light in its disbelief. "And I was shocked. Where did they come from? I thought this had been healed a long time ago. But, yeah, I started having all that. Everything just came late."

More than a decade late.

Elizah is sharp, sure, and sarcastic in the most subtle way. Barely thirty, she's built her own freelance business, working with virtual clients all over the world. She is at once a freckled, curly-haired free spirit (living in Costa Rica now, Ireland before that, another European city next) and a precise, exact professional. It's easy to imagine why her clients love her: her genuine desire to get it right. The way any time you talk to her, you can tell she's having the conversation with her whole heart.

When she was sixteen, she was raped. Then, again at twenty-six. She accepts that because of probability, she simply had a chance. She was never taken out of the equation. But that acceptance doesn't mean the trauma didn't compound.

After the first time, Elizah found justice in movie tickets.

A junior in high school, she wasn't allowed to sleep over at friends' houses. And that was the least of it. Having grown up in a religious household, she was familiar with the answer "no." Strict religion often tends to feel synonymous with the two-letter word: no sex before marriage, no eating certain foods, no work on the Holy day. But then, one night, Elizah's parents said "yes."

When it rains it pours: for a teenager, that cliché manifests as *when things are good, they're freaking awesome.* Elizah was excited to find out what happened at these mystical, girly-right-of-passage sleepovers she'd been barred from for so long. And then, as the teenage gods would have it, he texted her. *Want to go to the casino with me tonight? I have to drive my mom anyway, so we could hang out there while we wait.* Things went from good to freaking awesome.

Elizah didn't find out what happens at girly sleepovers that night. With her parents not expecting her back until the morning, she said "yes" to the casino, and "yes" to the invitation back to his parents' house when it eventually came. He offered her a drink (her first!), and she said "yes," after checking that his parents and little brother were home to make sure she was safe. He asked if she'd like to stay up late to watch a movie in the living room, and she said "yes" again. She was sixteen and taking full advantage of her one opportunity to be away from the watchful eyes of her parents. As the movie began to play, Elizah stopped saying "yes." But things kept happening.

Here's where Elizah's story parallels Isla's, from the beginning of the book. She had sex for the first time that night, without ever consenting to it.

Elizah didn't call it rape. Not at first. She woke up with a hazy memory, a bruise on her left knee from hitting the coffee table when he climbed on top of her, and a clear impression: she'd been mistreated. There was something sinister about the way she felt. It wasn't until years later that she'd learn, through a story from a friend, that casino boy had been on "a mission to collect as many virginities as he could."

That knowledge might have confirmed things for Elizah, and, at the very least, it could have given her experience a name. But without it, she wasn't sure what to do. Still having not identified it as "rape," reporting didn't cross her mind. Left with just an anger and discomfort that she couldn't quite pin down, she did what any teenager might do: blocked casino boy's number, and then also blocked him on every virtual platform she could. He was headed to college that fall, so if she wasn't seeing him online, she wasn't going to see him at all. It wasn't until a year later that she realized: she'd forgotten to block him on her Myspace account, the one with the fake name that she was sure he'd never find.

Elizah.

Elizah.

Elizah.

The incessant messages began a year later.

Why don't you talk to me anymore? Why did you block me on everything?

They pinged through her internet browser. She continued to ignore him, until—

Elizah, I know you're a Christian. And good Christians are supposed to forgive.

And that was it. A year later, Elizah had her proof: casino boy felt guilty. It wasn't just a weird feeling that she had in her gut. She had been mistreated that night.

"That's when I realized, 'Oh, shit, he just admitted it,'" she said, as passionately as if it were the day he'd pinged her. "He knows what he did because he's telling me that I need to forgive him. That's when I knew it wasn't just in my head, it happened to me. The fact that he had sort of confessed to it, in an indirect way, made me want to take action."

When Elizah takes action, she does so fiercely. It makes me smile to know she was always that way. Even—especially—at seventeen.

There's something so singularly beautiful about a woman on a mission—is there anyone as exuberantly powerful? Elizah must have been absolutely glowing that summer afternoon when she walked through the mall, scheme cooking in her seventeen-year-old brain, mane of burgundy-brown hair behind her. She was beelining for Baskin-Robbins.

Elizah had previously clocked that this boy was cute. Really cute. She didn't know him but had ordered ice cream from him a few times and knew he usually got off work right after the shop closed. Which, according to her mission, would be just about perfect timing.

"*Do you have a girlfriend?*" Elizah asked, brazenly. "*If you do, would she mind if I borrowed you for a fake date?*"

"I told him I needed to get back at someone," she explained, years later, "and he'd get a free movie out of it."

With the cute Baskin-Robbins employee locked into his role, Elizah set the rest of the plan in motion. She messaged casino boy.

"*You're right. I should forgive. Let's meet up and talk about it. Maybe let's do a movie date?*"

And a slightly shocked casino boy agreed, perhaps relieved of some of his guilt. Maybe smiling, thinking that what he'd done to her wasn't so unforgivable, after all. He showed up to the date that evening ready to pay for her ticket. It's the least he could do.

Meanwhile, the wheels of teenage justice were finally spinning for Elizah. She had casino boy right where she wanted him: happy. She had the Baskin-Robbins employee stationed inconspicuously on a bench outside the theater, and, to tie a literal bow on the whole event, she had a letter. Addressed to casino boy, explaining that she knew exactly what he'd done to her, sealed, wrapped in tissue paper, and tucked into a gift bag (she wanted it to seem like an innocent little gift, at first, nothing more).

"I waited for him to arrive, and when he did come, he came bounding into the theater like he owned the place," Elizah remembered. "He looked a little older, more mature, radiating that college-boy confidence. His hair was down to his shoulders, he wore a brand-new leather jacket, he looked cleaned up and ready for a romantic date with the girl he stole her virginity from."

Trying to hold off his suspicion for what she was about to do, when he hugged her, she hugged back.

"I gave him a believable one," she said, "all along knowing I was hugging my rapist. It felt disgusting."

And this is where Elizah found fairness in movie tickets. After casino boy bought them, she asked to hold them for a minute. She never gave them back, but instead, handed him the gift.

"Here, this is for you, but don't open it until after. You can only see what's inside when I'm gone," she said.

"Oh. Then why are you giving it to me now?" he responded, probably even more confused than he had been when she suggested she'd forgive him.

Elizah stopped here and almost didn't go through with the rest. "I felt like the biggest asshole on the planet," she remembered, "and I either teared up or almost teared up ... but knew I had to do it. For *me*. Then I said it."

"Because I'm about to walk away."

Handing a movie ticket to the cute Baskin-Robbins employee who was conveniently located nearby, Elizah walked into the theater with him, leaving casino boy open mouthed and gifted with her "this-is-what-I-*really*-think-of-you" letter. At seventeen years old, she gave herself the justice she wanted.

A quirky, fun, classic teenage tale, sure—but this story is more than that. It's just one portrait of where we go when there is no system we can rely on. It's about the ingenuity of women, and how, as things stand currently, the majority of us trust ourselves to create the outcome we deserve more than we trust any measure of law enforcement.

A woman does it herself. Because she has to.

But that was how Elizah DIY-ed justice before she even knew to call her mistreatment "rape." A decade later, when it happened again, she knew. As opposed to being unconscious, this time she said "no" as it was happening. But she still didn't report.

"I knew that I'd get nowhere," she explained. "The whole town had vouched for this guy, which is why I trusted him in the first place. His dad was extremely wealthy—he was the mayor. So, I realized I didn't want to report and go through all that for nothing."

Instead, as her trauma compounded, Elizah simplified: she moved out of town. Hardly a fair outcome but, given the fact that there was no system that would turn up a more righteous result for her, it was the best she could do.

And here's the thing when it comes to sexual violence. What is a fair outcome, anyway?

When someone sticks a part of themselves inside a part of you, without your consent, what amount of time is appropriate for them to spend in a cell? How much community service must they complete to ensure they won't disregard another human being again?

Is that quantifiable?

It is already so unfair to be raped or assaulted and then have to spend your most crucial healing moments in a cold police station, or at a courthouse. The criminal justice system feels like being "raped all over again."[164] That's what Frances Andrade, the woman who had been raped from the headlines my freshman year of college, texted her friend days before she killed herself. But, maybe if it was proven that the perp would be prosecuted, maybe if Elizah hadn't known it was a losing battle from the very beginning—maybe then it would be worth people inflicting more injustice on themselves.

If a fair outcome was the norm, instead of the exception, perhaps more people would stick it out. But, in the sexual violence arena, our system is largely dysfunctional. So, why disrupt the healing process? Why allow the trauma to compound while trudging through the criminal justice system?

"Elizah, before you get that look on your face, let me explain." Elizah was on a video call with her PTSD therapist, discussing how she seemed detached from what happened to her years before, and years before that.

"She says that my detachment from it is actually protecting me from reliving the trauma," Elizah explained, "and that it's probably a good thing. Because I've talked to a lot of women who have experienced sexual assault, and I can share my story with them, without having to physically relive it."

"So maybe it's me seeing silver linings," she continued, "but I can't erase the fact that it happened. What I can do is turn it into something that I can use to connect with other people."

---

164 Amelia Gentleman, "Prosecuting Sexual Assault: 'Raped All over Again,'" *The Guardian*, April 13, 2013.

E. JEAN

E. Jean Carroll wrote her advice column for *ELLE* magazine for twenty-six years.

Some of her story is known—cold hard facts from the news, the Twitter-sphere, pop culture history. Other parts, less so.

For example, who's to say what E. Jean was wearing the first time she set foot in the *ELLE* offices? She signed her contract in 1993 with a chic pen name and an impressive resume, one that included an Emmy for writing on *Saturday Night Live*, among other things.[165] And she was a sophisticated, New York City-made fifty-year-old on her first day of employment.[166] So you might envision her in some sort of fashion-forward ensemble that is perfectly stylish without trying too hard to be trendy. A pantsuit, maybe, with heels, and her blonde ponytail pulled back with a scrunchie. It was the '90s, after all.

The '90s, after all, were publicly good to E. Jean. Her *ELLE* column, "Ask E. Jean," permeated New York City society right at its heart: by becoming famous with women in their twenties and thirties, all of whom were struggling with something (namely, men).[167] Flipping through her archives feels like stepping into the sexy, pink, New York City dream world that's so ubiquitous on TV. But E. Jean wasn't writing for the fictionalized New York elite. She was writing for the everywoman, the anywoman, firing them up with blunt honesty and good-humored frankness.

---

165 Bonnie Fuller, "E. Jean Carroll: 5 Things on Writer Facing off with Justice Dept. over Her Trump Rape Charge," *Hollywood Life by Bonnie Fuller*, September 8, 2020.

166 Joan Kelly Bernard, "ELLE's E. Jean Carroll Dishes Out Sassy but Sane Advice," *News & Record*, January 25, 2015.

167 Ibid.

"Feminists are just humans who don't want women treated like crap," she once wrote.[168]

The women she fearlessly led away from bad relationships, toxic friends, and questionable situations may have been the first to notice E. Jean, but television producers weren't far behind. Looking to expand upon the success of the "Ask E. Jean" column, they put her on the silver screen. Just a year after signing with *ELLE*, E. Jean had an hour-long show on NBC's cable network (which would later become MSN-BC).[169] *Ask E. Jean*, the TV show, graced airwaves nationwide from 1994–1996.[170]

Suddenly women could see their wise columnist and, I don't even have to imagine here, it must have been everything they'd hoped for. E. Jean is slender, polished, and speaks through a huge, toothy smile, even when what she's saying is not necessarily positive. She's compassionate and vaguely reminiscent of your cool aunt: the one who's single and hip and lives in the city, close enough to a hairdresser to get her bob blown out twice a week. E. Jean laughs easily and can return to a genuine, serious posture just as quickly. She wraps her long, thin fingers around a coffee cup when she's listening, and then throws them around empathically as she speaks. Most strikingly, though, there's a spark behind her heavily made-up eyes that gives her away. She's game for almost anything.

---

168 E. Jean Carroll, "Ask E. Jean: My Boyfriend and I Keep Getting into the Same Fight about Feminism," *ELLE*, June 16, 2016.

169 "This Day in History: July 4, 2012," TV Worth Watching, accessed February 19, 2021.

170 Ibid.

It's fitting, then, that when she met a famous young real estate tycoon in a Bergdorf Goodman in the mid-1990s, she was ready to play. To a point.[171]

Here's another place we don't have to guess about E. Jean's story. An instance where we know exactly what she was wearing: a black wool Donna Karan coatdress and four-inch, black, patent-leather high heels from Barney's. We know because she kept the dress these last twenty-four years. Never laundered, in the back of her closet.[172]

So, yes, E. Jean looked the epitome of vogue during what was perhaps her most supreme reign, the golden era for her frank wisdom. She ran into the tycoon by chance, as a TV star/well-known magazine writer and an alleged millionaire might. After greeting each other—*"You're that advice lady!"* and *"You're that real estate tycoon!"*—she helped him shop for a gift, per his request. After trying the handbag and hat section, he suggested lingerie. They picked out a one-piece bodysuit, and he haggled her to try it on. She, having a great sense of humor, didn't stop him as he led her to the dressing room, thinking she was going to turn the tables. She was scheming to make him put it on, over his pants.[173] Always game, she was playing along.

The minute they got to the dressing room, though, the game ended. Or it escalated. Or, really, it became completely un-officiated. The door swung shut, and the tycoon lunged at her. He kissed her despite her attempts to shove him off. E. Jean had advised all of New York City on their struggles

---

171 E. Jean Carroll, "Hideous Men Donald Trump Assaulted Me in a Bergdorf Goodman Dressing Room 23 Years Ago. But He's Not Alone on the List of Awful Men in My Life," *New York Magazine, The Cut,* June 21, 2019.

172 Ibid.

173 Ibid.

with men, but in this Bergdorf dressing room she was alone, struggling with a man that had made up his mind. He seized her arms, pushed her against a wall, and pulled down her tights. He put himself inside her. She tried stomping on his foot with her patent-leather heel, and then finally got her knee up high enough to wedge him off. She ran out of the dressing room.[174]

Again: people don't run from consensual sexual encounters.

The next story element we do have to imagine. How long E. Jean's struggle to decide whether to report went on. We do know how it started:

"I told two close friends," she recounts, in her book, *What Do We Need Men For? A Modest Proposal.* "The first, a journalist, magazine writer, correspondent on the TV morning shows, author of many books, etc., begged me to go to the police. *'He raped you,'* she kept repeating when I called her. *'He raped you. Go to the police! I'll go with you. We'll go together.'* My second friend is also a journalist, a New York anchorwoman. She grew very quiet when I told her, then she grasped both my hands in her own and said, *'Tell no one. Forget it! He has two hundred lawyers. He'll bury you.'"*[175]

And we do know that, for many years, she heeded the advice of that second friend. "Like many women who are attacked," E. Jean writes, "when I had the most to say, I said the least."[176]

"Receiving death threats, being driven from my home, being dismissed, being dragged through the mud ... never

---

174 Ibid.

175 Ibid.

176 Ibid.

sounded like much fun," she expands, explaining why she didn't want to report. "Also, I am a coward."[177]

We know that, for the twenty-four years E. Jean kept the tycoon's actions to herself, her career continued. Flourished, even. In 2003, her column was ranked one of the five best in the country by the *Chicago Tribune*.[178] She published three books between the years of 1995 and 2019 and created three successful websites, one of which—Greatboyfriends.com—Oprah called, "The best idea she's ever heard of."[179] If that's not making it in America, what is?

She advised young women on predators in her column, penning fierce quips like: "I'm proud of you for standing up. You have earned the rank of Assertive, First Class; and by exterminating Dr. Seedy McSpice-Up, you have earned the respect of women everywhere."[180] And, until 2019, we can imagine her life as somewhat status quo, as far as life for a staple of the NYC writing scene goes.

We know how it changed. All of it, instantaneously, in one day. She published an excerpt from her newest book, where she lists the "Most Hideous Men of Her Life." Talk about compounded trauma—E. Jean was able to write an entire book about the list that summed up hers. The famous tycoon is number twenty, and with his name, she details

177 Ibid.

178 Lucy Zawadi, "E. Jean Carroll Biography: Age, Trump Lawsuit, Is She Married?" *Legit*, September 2020.

179 E. Jean Carroll, "Ask E. Jean: The Evolution of Wooing," *ELLE*, August 26, 2013.

180 E. Jean Carroll, "Ask E. Jean: January 2007," *ELLE*, December 12, 2006.

their Bergdorf encounter. Plus, a confession: she hasn't had sex with anyone since.[181]

These days, New York's cool aunt E. Jean is back on TV. But these days, instead of inspiring a generation by talking about their lives, she's firing up the next by talking about her own. Age has allowed her to shed whatever softness she once saved for the camera. She's still blonde and still slender, but maybe a little more transparent, a little more blunt. When she speaks about the assault, there's no playfulness in her silences. When she looks down, these days, it's somber.

"I was perfectly happy never to come forward," she begins, in one video interview. "Never, never, never to say anything." She pauses, almost resting her head on her long fingers. She continues, "My reputation, my life, my livelihood are all online. They're not only online, they're on *the* line."[182]

"I watched sixteen women come forward," she adds, referencing the slew of other people who had also accused the tycoon of assault, at the time, "and then saw [him] turn it around, deny it, and then attack them brutally. I didn't want to do that, I didn't want to be dragged through the mucky."[183]

What changed? What moved E. Jean to the "reported" camp?

"In the last two years, women started to ask me, should I come forward? How can I sit there and receive these women who are telling me their story, and I'm sitting there silent?"[184]

181 E. Jean Carroll, "Hideous Men Donald Trump Assaulted Me in a Bergdorf Goodman Dressing Room 23 Years Ago. but He's Not Alone on the List of Awful Men in My Life," *New York Magazine, The Cut,* June 21, 2019.

182 *New York Magazine,* "E. Jean Carroll on the Aftermath of Publishing Her Story," June 24, 2019, video, 05:09.

183 Ibid.

184 Ibid.

On the plus side, the uptick of women asking E. Jean about sexual assault probably means more of us are asking about it in general. Conversation, in place of secretive shame, is an important step. But, on the downside, when E. Jean did report her own experience, it was not without distress.

"Advice-people say you will feel better if you come forward. That's not true. You will feel like you're doing a good thing, you will feel you're doing the right thing, you will feel that you're helping other women, but it is very, very painful."[185]

We know another, final part of E. Jean's story: it doesn't end with the pain. The tycoon denied the allegations, and, in response, E. Jean created her own justice. She sued him for defamation.[186]

"I am filing not just for me but for every woman who's been pinched, prodded, cornered, felt up, pushed against the wall, grabbed, groped, assaulted, and had spoken up only to be shamed, demeaned, disgraced, passed over for promotion, fired and forgotten," she captioned an Instagram. "I am filing this suit because [he] is not above the law!"[187]

And then, mere months after E. Jean filed in the name of those who have reported and watched their career crumble under the weight of their allegations, the unprecedented occurred. *ELLE* fired E. Jean.[188]

---

185 Ibid.

186 Roberta Smith, "In a Mattress, a Lever for Art and Political Protest," *The New York Times*, September 21, 2014.

187 E. Jean Carroll (@ejeancarroll1), "I am suing the President of the United States for Defamation…," Instagram photo, November 4, 2019.

188 Katherine Rosman and Jessica Bennett, "What Happened between E. Jean Carroll and ELLE Magazine?" *The New York Times*, February 21, 2020.

While the internet erupted (all those twenty-and-thirty-somethings that E. Jean advised in the '90s are now established fifty-somethings with Twitter and other public platforms at their fingertips), E. Jean kept it classy. Stylish, without trying too hard to be trendy. Honest and careful not to blame the wrong person.

"Because [the tycoon] ridiculed my reputation, laughed at my looks, and dragged me through the mud, after 26 years, *ELLE* fired me," she wrote. "I don't blame *ELLE*. It was the great honor of my life writing 'Ask E. Jean.' I blame [him]."[189]

The timing of E. Jean's departure from *ELLE* could raise questions: she went public with assault accusations in June 2019 and was fired eight months later. *ELLE* released a statement saying they are unrelated, but E. Jean (and her large following of supporters) seemingly disagree.[190] Inferences aside, though, the facts of her story remain the same.

She was assaulted in the heyday of her career, kept it a secret, continued building that career, and then reported. Not only has her employment status changed, post-report, but she also still has not received justice—or any type of admission of guilt—from the real-estate tycoon who assaulted her.

And as for the facts of the real estate tycoon's story? Perhaps most notably, he served as the forty-fifth president of the United States.

With sixteen accusations of assault and counting, Americans elected to put him in office.

Hardly a balanced, fair outcome.

---

189 Ibid.
190 Ibid.

STOP THE BLEEDING

---

*"In times of stress, the best thing we can do for each other
is to listen with our ears and our hearts and to be assured
that our questions are just as important as our answers."*

—MISTER ROGERS

On my twenty-second birthday, just shy of three years after
that indigo night in Boston, I wrote:

*At twenty-one, I moved three thousand miles from home.
When I got here with two suitcases, an upgraded rental car
(thanks to Denise who works the 4:00 a.m. shift at Enterprise),
and a five-week long job, I was pretending.*

*"I'm here to work in TV," I'd tell people in suits. "I'm here
to work on my Instagram," I'd quip to new friends. "I'm just
here for a couple of years to explore," I'd assure myself.*

*I arrived West with scarred feet. Not even scarred, really.
Openly wounded. I could never figure out where the cuts came from,
but they were fleshy and loud and impossible to cover completely.*

*But this year, my first West-Coast birthday is gifting me a
new, maybe grown-up, knowledge. Life leaves scrapes on feet.
At least, on any feet worth having. Keep using them to run.*

This morning I sprinted to the Pacific Ocean like it was getting impatient for me. I slipped out of my sneaks and into the tide and let waves wash over and over and over, grabbing my ankles. The Pacific does two things to open wounds, I've learned. It numbs them, and then it heals them.

You can get so caught up in moving cross-country and letting the waves hit you, that you don't even notice scrapes fading. Until one day, maybe on your twenty-second birthday, you look down and they're gone.

Newly twenty-two years old, for what might have been the first time in three years, I sensed proof of healing.

*

"Healing" is one of those words, though, that's hard to quantify while it occurs. A process much easier to understand in hindsight.

And even in hindsight, healing has gotten murky for the average American consumer. Was it the antidepressants that made the difference, or the crystals? This self-help book with a swear in the title, or that other one? At best, healing remains the practice of becoming healthy again. At worst, it's a stock image of a ball of light between two hands, implying there is some final, fully healed destination to seek.

To be clear, I bought into it. Still do! Inspirational quotes and rose quartz can do wonders for a heart, and a horoscope can make you feel less alone. For a while, when I went West, I thought of the Pacific as a sacred solution. Between its tides, I changed. I was sure of it.

But, in hindsight, it wasn't the Pacific. It was focus on it, presence in it. It was standing still in nature, watching everything continue to push and pull around me. And while healing is an elusive term, not an achievement, by the end of that first Californian year I felt like I was floating in that realm. The faded scrapes were evidence.

A medical professional (or a professional-looking medical website, in this case) will explain the following about cuts and scrapes: "Wounds heal in stages. The smaller the wound, the quicker it will heal. The larger or deeper the wound, the longer it takes to heal."[191]

The website will go on to tell you about the first two to five days. The tender period. The scrape swells, becomes red or pink, and a scab forms. Not something to pick at. [192]

Like those red summer months. In the first few days, my eyes can't finish a smile. The heat torments me for weeks, but I collect my old friend MK, my summer-crush Liam, and many, many women around me. I'm hurt, but they keep any more pain from getting in. They protect my wound from infection, during that tender period.

Tissue growth and rebuilding happen next, the website goes on to say. Around the three-week mark, new skin begins to form.[193]

Like when I return to Boston, somehow only a summer older than I left it. I'm okay, and that's empowering. My new skin feels tough and radiant.

And scarred. The next step, for flesh wounds, is scar formation. This happens because new skin tissue grows back differently. The scar will be smaller than the original wound, less strong and less flexible than the area around

191 "How Wounds Heal," Medicine Plus, accessed February 19, 2021.

192 Ibid.

193 Ibid.

it. It takes time for the spot you were scraped to return to full functionality.[194]

Take dating after, for example. Explaining why you want to wait on just about everything. At first, it's clunky, a barely understandable jumble of loose, quiet words. Then it smooths out: vulnerable, well-practiced. And then, maybe, you stop needing to wait.

Scars can take up to two years to fade completely. Some never do. The deeper the wound, the more likely you are to have a lasting scar. In the world of flesh wounds, that is.[195]

Sexual violence cuts deep. It's hard to measure when and if its scars ever fade completely.

This is a book, not a medical manual. But our bodies—our first and final homes—are the ultimate teachers. Assault and rape invade them physically, but often the longest-lasting cut they leave is emotional. Turns out, recovery of any kind isn't all that different.

Muscles and bones heal similarly: through destruction, repair, and remodeling. If you break a bone or sprain a muscle, you're likely put in a brace or cast. You might be handed crutches. The reason? To increase immobilization and decrease the amount of weight you're putting on the injury. Together, focus and stillness minimize pain and jumpstart healing. After a bone split, even the slightest movement of the broken part will delay the healing process. Bearing any type of weight is strictly forbidden. In fact, if you put pressure on a busted bone too soon, it's detrimental.[196]

---

194 Ibid.

195 Ibid.

196 Brian Whittington, "Understanding the 3 Phases of Muscle Healing," *Athletico Physical Therapy*, March 27, 2017.

Sexual violence is no different. No matter how you qualify it, that person is either wounded, injured, or shattered.

When we are recovering physically, professionals demand rest and immobility and ban weight-bearing and picking at scabs. When we are recovering from sexual violence, the opposite is too often true.

Think about it: in the immediate aftermath of one of the most serious emotional wounds people can incur, they are expected to move. The professionals who aid in their recovery put the onus on the injured to get to and from a police station, an office, a hospital. The newly broken are asked to bend and stretch to make an accusation—often, we need to jump around just to be noticed. *This is serious,* we have to insist. *He shattered me. You can't see it, but I am wounded.*

As the system currently exists, pressing charges demands a person exert every bit of their energy. While still in the early phases of healing, they bear all kinds of weight. They should be given room to be immobile, if that's what they want. Instead, they are forced to relive the sexual violence story before officers, committees, a judge, and a jury. *Act fast,* statutes of limitations taunt. *Provide more evidence,* systems of every kind insist.

Healing is an intangible term, especially for people who have experienced sexual violence. No two restorative paths look the same. But the consistencies with our own natural patterns are a good place to start. In the wake of the wound, let fragments reconnect, let scabs form. Leave space for stillness. And remember, that person is not in a place to be picked at.

*

Intentional forfeit of control was never a practice I was good at, but as Oprah and my mom and any spiritual guide will tell you, it feels good. There is beauty in purposeful surrender. In choosing to throw up your hands, throw away schedules, and let life find you. Giving up control can be liberating, yes. But having control taken from you? Imprisoning.

When you are assaulted or raped, it feels like you are thrown into a jail cell of sorts.

Your cries of innocence and insistence that you don't want to be there do nothing to save you. The jailer didn't even listen to your original "no." From the outside, it may seem that when the attack is over, the prison door swings open. You're free to walk out. But, as long as a person continues to feel unheard, they remain trapped. People don't just walk back into their control, after an assailant takes it from them. Someone needs to hand it back. And then it needs to be handed back over and over and over again, pressed into the hands of the person who lost it.

Control is taken for minutes, hours. We might need months, years to believe it's ours again.

After experiencing sexual violence, there is no road map for healing. But if there were, the center point would be control. Regained control and then, another key coordinate: dissolution of shame.

Shame is a persistent, intrinsic belief that you are bad. It sticks to a person's insides like tar, dripping through their body until their core is coated in *I-am-not-worthy*s. Shame suffocates self-esteem and stunts any type of healing. It goes beyond simple guilt, which is more like an internal flood of *I-did-something-bad*s. A flood washes away. Tar sticks. And tar poisons.

After a person experiences sexual violence, they fight to find a way back to their control. Back to their power of choice. They're out of the prison they were put in, but if they lug around internal shame with them, they might not get very far. Tar-coated organs are heavy; shame is the ultimate weight.

Brené Brown, psychologist and researcher, famously found that the antidote to shame is vulnerability.[197] Her viral TEDx Talk explains how we can dissolve shame by sharing that which we hide, and being met with acceptance. Only when we feel safe, when shame is off the table, is there room for what we most deeply seek: connection.

And that's where I landed, after several warm, genuine conversations with the women in this book—conversations that were at once both delicate and impassioned, biting and hopeful. Surrounded by blueprints, rolled out all over paper scraps and word docs, I sat down to write with renewed reverence for human connection.

Deep in the sovereignty of that connection, I felt free to examine our system unforgivingly. I was also free to examine the varied threads of healing—how, eventually, they all knot together. Ultimately, though, I found myself caped in a hair salon one afternoon with my laptop open and a dazed expression when the stylist asked, *What does the book really examine?* I trailed into some combination of *Um, well, I guess—Sounds like it's about sharing stories,* she shrugged.

The power of shared story. That is what it's about. That's what it's always been about, since those summer nights on the front porch decades ago. Shared story is the safe space where shame dies. The expansive world where we can see clearly we aren't alone in any pain, and we never have been. Shared story shows us how: at a young age, I heard it guide my mom through maintaining a healthy marriage, my aunt

---

197 Technology, Entertainment, Design, "The Power of Vulnerability | Brené Brown," January 3, 2011, video.

through managing demanding days at work, and even my grandmas through troubleshooting those damn desktop computers. Shared story can show us how much we're worth, how to get where we want to go, and, most vitally, shared story shows us how to heal.

When stories remain unspoken, it's harder to maneuver healing. It's easy to know what not to do: don't move, don't pick scabs, don't rush yourself (all actions that are difficult to avoid when a person chooses to report). But we're left without its counter. "What to do?" That lives in story.

Without a usable system to direct them or stories to show them how, the women in this book were able to steer through shame and back to control on their own. Ayana worked with her therapist and when she got to college, made a name for herself. Naomi boldly bought a one-way ticket cross-country, and, in four years, is infinitely more successful than the problematic CEO.

Rachel gave herself a choice: how accountable would she hold locker-mate? She made the powerful decision to let it slide. To protect him from his own actions. Her return to control came in the form of mercy.

Isla created fearlessly, and in the poetry she shares today, reveals a forceful vulnerability. Gracie is unashamed, deciding with care how and when and with whom her story is shared.

Each of these women became a cartographer. They navigated their way into the elusive process of healing without a clear path before them. So many of us do. But I couldn't help but wonder, how much less painful could the process have been if they had that "how to"? There is no road map for healing, but there could be.

After phone calls and research and a news cycle that continued to reveal even more instances of previously-unreported sexual assault, I was left with more than just reverence and wonder. It was clear: the front porch is full to capacity with people who have experienced sexual violence—even my editor had a story to share. But I couldn't shake the feeling that, although the front porch feels massive and packed, it is small compared to legislation, government, and the unwelcoming powers that be.

These stories, in their unreported magnitude, sketch out the system we would report to. They're a draft, a map of healing that law enforcement needs to avoid obstructing at all costs. The message these stories spin needs to swell off the front porch and soar down the street (carried there by sea salt winds) all the way up through systems and establishments until change happens. It is imperative. But that's a long way for words.

I felt a little hopeless. And then I met Carrie Hull.

NOTHING IS FOR
EVERYONE

———

"The facade has to drop. The 'I'm a cop,' all that kind of stuff has to drop. You just are who you are. And that's a scary thing for a lot of people. But it's necessary."

—*DAVID LISAK*

"I think I love you," Senator Claire McCaskill said frankly, lighting up C-SPAN airwaves across the country.[198]

You didn't have to be there to know the chamber's staleness and dingy smell. Telegraphed over public access static, a group of eleven people in business-casual attire were dutifully taking turns delivering their final remarks. This group of experts was gathered for the Sexual Assault on College Campuses roundtable hosted by Senator McCaskill in the summer of 2014, and while the information they delivered was ultimately hopeful, the setting was downright drab.

———

198 C-Span, "Sexual Assault on College Campuses," June 23, 2014, video.

Among them? Carrie Hull. To me, she was the key.

To the rest of the world, she was a detective from the Ashland, Oregon police department. That day, she concluded her turn deliberately, in a low, urgent tone. She described significantly reformed law enforcement agencies, and how they could play an integral role not only in receiving reports, but in preventing sexual violence altogether.

"When you break from the traditional model of law enforcement, and you start providing an environment that encourages reporting, and therefore identifying serial perpetrators ... that is a form of prevention." Low ponytail firmly in place, Carrie's hands gestured across the table as she continued to explain, emphasizing each point. "We are not only sending a message to victims that they should be heard ... we're sending a message to offenders—"

"That's right," said the senator, unable to withhold her admiration. I was right there with her.

"That they can no longer keep people silent in the same way they have before," finished Carrie. It was then that Senator McCaskill professed her love, and a laugh rolled through the once-dull chamber.[199]

Six summers later, the COVID-19 pandemic was the only headline. Zoom conferences replaced roundtables, sweat suits replaced office wear, and for many (me included), parents' houses replaced small city apartments. The world was unrecognizable, compared to that dull summer 2014 conference, let alone compared to Isla's summer, years earlier. But at least this time, it was all going down to the tune of two Taylor Swift album releases.

That afternoon, sitting in my childhood bedroom, I paused the clip and Googled: "Detective Carrie Hull."

---

199 Ibid.

*

By the time I dialed Carrie's number, I'd nailed down a few absolute "needs," for any system that's designed to help a person in the aftermath of sexual violence. Healing remained primo, but it was also elusive (and it continues to be). A few contributing factors to healing, though, were more simply defined. Control and vulnerability, for example. But also, safety.

Safety exists in the acceptance of those you tell. It's in their gentleness and their empathy and, sometimes, it's in their outrage on your behalf. It's in each of the small ways their reactions dissolves shame. But safety also comes from not seeing your story in headlines and from being able to keep your work life separate and successful. It's born out of involving your family how and when you want to, sparing yourself months of legal turmoil, and, occasionally, from choosing not to harm another—even if that "other" is your assailant.

As it stands right now, systems don't provide safety. But Carrie figured out a way that they could.

In 2009, she decided to tackle the mysterious, under-reported crime of sexual violence.[200] She started in the same place this book does: by asking people for their stories. Methodically, she compiled her research. Every single interviewee answered uniquely in terms of why they didn't report, what made them hesitant to report, or what they wish was different about the law enforcement system. No two answers were the same, and yet: every single person she spoke with cited confidentiality as crucial. For many, it's the differentiating factor between approaching the police and going unreported.

---

200 "About Us," You Have Options Program, accessed February 19, 2021.

The solution, here? The anonymous report.

If anonymous reporting sounds radical, that's because when it comes to sexual assault, it is. But it's accepted, if not encouraged, when it comes to other crimes.

"You probably cannot think of a jurisdiction in the United States that would turn away anonymous information on somebody who's selling drugs in that town," Carrie explained to me during our phone interview. "I worked drug cases very early in my career ... we worked with a lot of confidential informants, and we paid people for information. You know, got into a car, brought somebody in, gave them money to go buy drugs so that we could get intel on who was causing problems in our community. So if that's allowed—if you can literally pay people for information about criminal activity in the area—in what way can we not accept an anonymous report about a potential perpetrator of sexual violence?"

Armed with her knowledge of other crime and interview results that showed how confidentiality could make all the difference, Carrie created the You Have Options Program. The first time I looked at its website, I got chills. *Someone figured it out.*

"The goal [of You Have Options] is to create an environment where victims of sexual assault are in complete control and able to share their experience without fear or pressure," the landing page reads. "Understanding that each person has unique needs and barriers when reporting to law enforcement, YHOP agencies acknowledge that justice is not the same for everyone."[201]

That more or less translates to this: YHOP makes reporting accessible. What a simple, powerful idea.

---

201 "Explore Your Options," You Have Options Program, accessed February 19, 2021.

So here's how it works: first, a law enforcement agency chooses to become affiliated with YHOP, signing up for vigorous training and reform. Ultimately, what they're signing up for is to give people who have experienced sexual violence exactly what the name of the program might lead you to believe: options. Law enforcement agencies that participate in YHOP offer three different ways to report: information only, partial investigation, or full investigation. Reporting choice, though, is just the first of 20 "elements" the program sets in place.[202]

Number two? "A victim or other reporting party may remain anonymous and still have the information they provide documented by a law enforcement agency."[203]

As Carrie explained in the chamber that summer six years ago, and then again to me on the phone, people get lost when they conflate an original anonymous report with any kind of persecution. The process she designed is about intelligence, not accusation. An anonymous report does not deem the reported assailant a suspect. It does not necessarily equate to action against them. The report just provides valuable intel to law enforcement—the same kind of intel they're already gathering when it comes to other types of threats within a community.

In other words, these programs provide the type of officially documented intel that might have allowed Dr. Christine Blasey Ford to prove her case to the Senate Judiciary Committee, while still enjoying the safety that confidentiality granted her in the decades before that trial began.

But Carrie isn't focused on thirty-six years later, when someone's grown up boy assailant is nominated to become a

---

202 Ibid.

203 Ibid.

Supreme Court Justice. She's not focused on any point down the line, really. Her goal—one of them, at least—is to educate law enforcement agencies on how to increase accessibility to people who have experienced sexual violence. If a person chooses to remain fully anonymous, there might be limits to what law enforcement can do with that information, but at least they have it. Of course, Carrie laughed, this all comes with very real obstacles.

"As an officer, your role is to collect information—that's how you do an investigation," she said. "Where it gets complicated for people is not so much legally can you do it, [but when] they start bringing morals and ethics into it. And they start confusing, you know, all of the just procedure with, 'Well maybe we shouldn't'. And that's the problem."

I asked Carrie what kind of morals and ethics would make an officer think, "Well, maybe we shouldn't." She said that, in her most candid conversations with members of law enforcement, they speak to their fear of false reports. Carrie calls it, "the myth" of false reporting.

"It's so fascinating," she began, "because if you actually look at the research, *way* more people, even when I was on patrol, would report their car being stolen falsely than would falsely report sexual violence. And so, if you look at the actual data, the fear of false reporting makes no sense. But people aren't interested in actual data, really. It's not that interesting. What is more interesting is the anecdote that somebody says their friend was falsely accused and it ruined his or her life."

And she's right. A false report does have the power to smear a name, trash a reputation. Even if a person is ultimately charged not guilty, the report alone can be enough to create wreckage. If reporting was more accessible, it might follow that the number of false reports would increase. But, using the YHOP model, there is space between the original report and any potential next steps. That space is for the person reporting to decide on their next move, yes, but also, it's for law enforcement to evaluate the case.

As Carrie put it, "just because somebody can use a tool inappropriately or illegally doesn't mean you take the tool away from everybody. Your professional job is to be able to figure that out."

While Carrie spoke, I scribbled notes on the back of that day's to-do list—new ideas to ask her about, if-then hypotheses to run by her. This was huge—she was outlining a system that would protect women in this book in the same way their unreports had. I was enthralled, and unsurprisingly my scrap of paper was full after fewer than fifteen minutes. Careful to move at a decibel that wouldn't be picked up on the phone, I frantically dropped to my stomach, peeking under the bed. Between "mmm-hmm"s and "yeah"s, I slid a box out from under it. An overlooked plus side of the pandemic? Plenty of half-finished journals at your disposal when you get furloughed and move home.

I flipped open the one on top. *Yikes.* An old journal entry about litmus testing from 2018 glared back at me: *Sometimes a circumstance is just plain acidic,* it began. I didn't let myself get any further, rifling to an unmarked page in the journal and back to my conversation with Carrie. After months of research, I was unprepared for the ways she was making me think, and for the new points she raised.

Carrie was explaining a lunch she had with a city council member. Listening to her, it became clear for the first time: there's a difference between the "professional jobs" law enforcement officers are given, and the roles they ultimately play in a community. They are employed to keep a place safe, but their work is also essential in keeping it desirable.

Think about the process of moving to a new neighborhood. When you're scoping out different spots online, you might check the median age, average income, cost of living. You might research stats on the local schools. And, at some point, you are almost definitely going to Google the crime rate.

Imagine that number is high. You look into it, and a page populates with headlines that express concern over high rates of sexual violence. Obviously, a "con" for that community.

What those headlines aren't saying is that high numbers of assaults actually reflect a higher rate of reporting. The community isn't necessarily rampant with predators, the police department might just be effectively encouraging people who have experienced sexual violence to come forward. Chances are, the police are doing something right, not wrong.

In another interview I conducted, Ashley Anstett, a criminal justice coordinator on Oregon's Sexual Assault Task Force, explained that when Oregon's numbers skyrocketed, she saw it as a good thing. "Last time I checked, we were number two in the country for reporting rates. Technically, we were number two for the highest amount of sexual assault," she clarified. "But I attribute that ranking to higher reporting rates because we have created systems that survivors feel comfortable coming forward to."

But that doesn't change the fact that politicians and law enforcement in the state have to explain articles that are ominously titled with the completely unnuanced: "Report: Oregon Has Very High Rate of Female Sexual Assault."[204]

And that's why Carrie takes city council members to lunch. Over sandwiches and salads, she explains that beneath

---

204 Chris Lehman, "Report: Oregon Has Very High Rate of Female Sexual Assault," *OPB*, September 21, 2016.

the potentially harmful clickbait titles, high reporting is something to be proud of. Plus, she says, the spike should only be temporary because of that fateful truth: If a rapist isn't stopped, they will, on average, commit the crime five more times.[205]

If they are stopped, then? Potentially five fewer cases of sexual assault.

*

Carrie likes her job. It's a caveat she often leads with.

"We have an amazing amount of people in the profession that are in it to do the right thing," she began, on an NPR interview with Terry Gross.[206] But, she then proceeds to say the nature of law enforcement is one of the most challenging obstacles she's encountered.

It really comes down to that first moment, she told me. The initial collision between the person reporting sexual violence, and the police officer taking the report. In that moment, the juxtaposition between how law enforcement operates and how healing unfolds is painfully prominent. There is no crossover.

Police don't interview effectively, Carrie explains. It's an issue that stems from both training and authority.

"Throughout my career, I absolutely came from a place where my profession told me we knew what was right," she said. There was no part of her training that encouraged anything but the directive that police are to command. The

205 David Lisak and Paul M. Miller, "Repeat Rape and Multiple Offending among Undetected Rapists," *Violence and Victims,* 17, no. 1, (February 2002)

206 "About Us," You Have Options Program, accessed February 19, 2021.

moment an officer is sworn in, they are vested with power that they are not made to feel is theirs to give up.

What happens when an officer sits down with a person reporting sexual violence, then? A person whose healing demands that the officer give some of their power away. How does the officer reconcile their vested control with the feeling they need to share it? To press some of it back into the palms of the person in front of them.

"I don't think that there is a lot of victim interviewing taught in the academy," Ashley told me. "There are some really phenomenal organizations that teach forensic interviewing and trauma informed forensic interviewing, but it's specialized, it's not part of the day-to-day. And so what happens is officers interview victims like they would interview a suspect."

A suspect might be met with suspicion, which is devastating for a person who has just been assaulted or raped. A suspect might be interviewed without empathy, camaraderie, or ceded control. But to interview a recently assaulted person that way? There's a real possibility that could dangerously stunt her healing process. Instead, she needs to have her vulnerability accepted, honored. Her shame reduced.

Of course, reducing shame is an art. Untrained, it's not one officers usually think to master. Often, as Carrie explains, just by refusing to hand control over to the person reporting, they increase that person's level of shame. "That's where all our assumptions really lie," she said, "trying to say, you know, 'Here's the solution and shame on you if you don't take it because we put all this work into making a solution for you.'"

*

David Lisak knows about wrongful shame. A clinical psychologist whose research focuses on rape and abuse, David, was sexually abused as a child. In an effort to help other men avoid the isolating shame he experienced, David founded the Bristlecone Project: a compilation of 140 stories from men who have experienced sexual violence. Their stories, posted online for others to see, are integrated with a larger organization. An organization called "1in6," named for the fact that one in every six men has an experience that could qualify them as a member.[207]

When I got off the phone with Carrie, he was my next dial.

"The vast majority of survivors of any kind of sexual violence experience severe and completely misplaced shame," he began, his voice piercingly honest. "I'm acutely aware of how our shame manifests and how shame cripples lives, and it's really tragic." For men who have experienced sexual violence, especially, David found that shame sticks for years, weighing men down until they are submerged in it.

Men are no exception to the unreported rule. Like their female counterparts, they understand the system is broken, and so, they opt out. David points to the very nature of police interviews as a primary example of how ineffective the system is for those who have been assaulted. "The first inhibition against reporting," he told me, "is that when somebody has been harmed in that way that's profoundly intimate and personal, they just really want to be left alone. You don't want to talk. And lord, you don't want to talk to a stranger. You don't want to talk to anyone who is remotely disconnected. You need to talk to someone who can show genuine compassion."

Compassion is a muscle. If you don't flex it often, it will deteriorate, leaving you weak. But what about police officers

207 Homepage, 1in6, accessed February 19, 2021.

who were trained to lift without that muscle group altogether? Police officers who were instructed to pump authority and lawfulness instead of "soft" emotions? Police officers who (and this is important) would have much harder jobs if they flexed compassion all the time. Where do they end up when they're asked to use a limp muscle?

Maybe, they pretend. A tactic David scoffs at.

"If you sit down with me and you think you're going to pretend to be genuine," he said, frankly, "that's not going to work. And when you're sitting across from somebody who is profoundly traumatized, who is highly emotional, they're going to detect a lack of genuineness even faster."

They might not get it from law enforcement, but genuineness is one of the main attractions for the men that join the "1in6" network. They join it for true understanding, for real compassion. They join to experience the power of shared story, and in the midst of pages of virtual testimonials, they make a realization: they aren't alone in their pain. They never were.

David speaks slowly, almost whimsically, like he's wandering from one intellectual thought to the next. As we wandered together on the phone that afternoon, we eventually approached new territory: masculinity. Masculinity is, like healing, one of those elusive, hard-to-define terms. In her book, *For Love of Men*, Liz Plank gets pretty close. She describes it as "the pressure to never show vulnerability or [be] emotional, this idea that boys will be boys, [that they] are rougher and tougher and are created differently than girls."[208] This pressure against vulnerability is part of the reason men don't report—part of the reason they often don't

---

208 Renee Morad, "Liz Plank: Why Traditional Masculinity Remains a Barrier for Us All," *NBC News, Know Your Value,* January 8, 2021.

tell anyone about assault. But the pressures of masculinity also contribute directly to the issues with law enforcement.

"There is rampant, bone-deep hostility toward vulnerability everywhere," David said. "Everybody, and every institution, even the practices that make up the criminal justice system." I asked him what that hostility meant for people who had experienced sexual assault and violence.

"It means it is possible to have a non-traumatizing experience when you report sexual assault," he answered, "But for that to happen, you'd have to have the luck of the ages."

*

After speaking to the experts, I spent a long afternoon just absorbing. Pages of my old journal freshly filled and sprawled in front of me, I was struck. The people who had devoted their lives to this work already had the solutions. They were well aware of the inherent flaws in the reporting system. They knew that police protocols did not properly account for bias, compassion, or for the fact that sexual violence is bigger than crime. It's injury. In their words, fixing these problems sounded simple—Carrie had already designed an entire program! Why, then, were more effective protocols still not in place?

I frowned for a couple of days, eyebrows furrowed, running through the same question in my head: If all this info was already out there, why didn't law enforcement get it by now? And then I remembered something Ashley had shared with me. A fact that, in hindsight, felt sinister.

In some cases, law enforcement is sensitive to the fact that trauma doesn't play by a rule book. They concede it can't exist in one straight, predetermined series. When there is an officer-involved shooting, for example, many police departments make it a policy to wait forty-eight hours before even taking a statement. As Ashley explained, "that's just because they know the brain needs time to sleep and process that information."

So, law enforcement does change the rules—they do, sometimes, bend under the weight of trauma. When it's one of their own, they get it. Why then, when it's a freshly-assaulted person reporting, do they forget?

My confusion was tinged with a little bit of fury now. A popular refrain came to mind, one that's been echoed across thought pieces all over the internet. What if the system wasn't broken, but rather, working exactly as it was intended to?

*

And I'm an optimist! I want to believe in society. I want to believe that our systems are designed for good. But, as the pandemic continued its hold on 2020, it was becoming almost impossible to maintain that belief.

Summer unfurled and found me writing, on unemployment, looking for jobs in case my old one decided not to bring me back. Like the rest of the world, I was disoriented and upset. With each new week that COVID-19 numbers climbed, the disorient and upset sank deeper into my body. But nothing sent those emotions plummeting through my soul quite like the memory of the final exchange from my conversation with Carrie.

She left me with a generalization and I couldn't shake it: it is known that law enforcement is "particularly bad," when it comes to handling sexual violence as a crime. "But," she continued, "that isn't to say that we are particularly great at other ones."

"Nobody is going to be able to build something that works for everybody," she said, "and it's such a privileged and frankly just ridiculous thing to think that. And that is the justice system, by the way."

I'd spent months trying to answer a fairly localized set of questions: why isn't everyone reporting sexual assault and rape? In what ways does our system prevent people from doing so? Carrie challenged that problem, broadening it.

"I actually think at an individual level, you have the exact same barriers to entry with reporting rape that you have across all crimes," she said. "You have shame, you have fear … humans are pretty consistent with the things that make them hesitant to report. And that is just true across the board."

All that is wrong with our system, for people who have been raped or assaulted, is also wrong just for people in general. I was dislodged by this realization.

Law enforcement is not working, not for the majority of Americans. In vastly different ways, the system is ultimately the same: tragically and undeniably ineffective. It's frightening to consider that the system put in place to protect an entire country could be beyond flawed: unusable, even fatal. That should implore us to demand: fix it. It should inspire us to be unprecedented: in thinking, in creation. And, soul-deep, it should scare us all.

Even the optimists.

YOU'RE INVITED

"I think being brave, in the face of a sexual assault, shouldn't be, 'Well if you reported, that's your medal of bravery.' For some people, to wake up every day and put their feet on the floor and not want to crawl back into bed and die is brave."

—JENNA STARK

The next step was, obviously, seeing a therapist.

Of course, this call was under the guise of a book interview. But I hoped she might also inadvertently help me with the disorient and upset that I was grappling with—the same feeling much of the country was wading through too. Turns out, that soul-deep assault on my optimism was a lens-changer.

Jenna Stark, LCSW, LICSW, picked up the phone with a smile. Her voice is the kind that you can just tell she's smiling, but also, I knew from experience. I used to see Jenna (in actual sessions, not just book interviews) while I worked on the show with the fake rain. And, while she power walked the beachy Santa Monica boardwalk and I sat at a makeshift desk in my childhood bedroom, we broke things down.

Before opening her own talk therapy practice in Los Angeles ("Braver Living"), Jenna was a therapist on staff at a university in Boston. I wondered if, had I decided to report, our paths might have crossed there. But then, Boston's a small city full of big campuses. Campus sexual assault and violence is rampant all over, and city schools in the Bean are no exception. From what Jenna described to me, she had enough on her plate just dealing with one campus.

Jenna's work with people who have experienced sexual violence didn't end when she left that Boston campus. We're everywhere. Well practiced in "what comes after," she shared some insight on healing that hadn't turned up in my research.

"You might have heard of the phases of grief," she began.

"Right, of course" I said, while flipping open my laptop to Google "what are the phases of grief?" As she spoke, the search results populated: denial and isolation, anger, bargaining, depression, and finally, acceptance.[209]

"I actually think people who have been sexually assaulted follow the same steps," she continued. "Grief happens when the world is never going to be the same. When someone is sexually assaulted, it's very much the same reaction of 'I can't believe this happened,' or 'that didn't happen.' It's the denial that their story has forever been changed by somebody else. That they didn't have a choice, and that their control was taken."

Grief phases aren't exact, Jenna explained, but in the early aftermath of tragedy, while a scab is still forming, they offer comforting structure. It was hard not to try to fit myself into them, as she listed. Some stages were easy to pinpoint, looking back at that indigo Boston night and everything that

---

209 Julie Axelrod, "The 5 Stages of Grief & Loss," *Psych Central*, May 17, 2016.

unfolded after. Others, less so. And then she mentioned new research that suggests a sixth phase. A final destination after the final destination, for healing: meaning making.

"Through meaning, we can find more than pain," says David Kessler, in his book that explains the sixth stage.[210] "Finding meaning in loss empowers us to find a path forward. Meaning helps us make sense of grief."

Meaning-making can "take many shapes," Kessler goes on to explain.

Maybe it takes the shape of a 210-page book.

Jenna kept talking and power walking. I wondered what other boardwalkers might think, if they caught wind of our conversation; a unique combo of self-help style buzzwords like "healing" and "support" and "bravery," contrasted with "rape," "assault," and "trauma." But that's the nature of the topic. Very dark, and then, somehow, light.

"In my experience," Jenna said, toward the end of our conversation, "women do not get unstuck until radical acceptance happens. Radical acceptance is saying, 'Okay, this happened to me. I don't have to like it. I don't have to agree with it. But it doesn't change the fact that this happened, and this is now a part of my story.' Or, as I like to say to patients, it's part of your patchwork quilt. It's just one patch of the quilt, and it does not have to define you by any means, but to pretend it didn't happen can cause long-term damage."

Jenna assured me that, while the stages of grief are a guideline and radical acceptance is a tentpole, there are infinitely more pieces to any given person's healing puzzle. Support groups, for example, are one she often suggests. They're

---

210 David Kessler, *Finding Meaning: The Sixth Stage of Grief* (New York: Scribner, 2019), 2.

empowering, she explained, because it's "helpful to hear others' stories. Someone else's story is your survival guide."

This all may sound a little mystical wellness industry-esque. But then it's you. And suddenly, you realize why every cliché about healing became cliché in the first place: because it put words to some universal truth. It's you, and other people's stories matter more than they ever had before. They become a place of solace, of connection, of "how to." When it's you, you feel just how significant it is to simply hear another's story.

*

This book was not a topic of conversation around our house—not often. With five adults living, working, and doing college from home, we were all pretty committed to our Zoom schedules. Plus, the topic was an uncomfortable kind of sad, so I didn't bring it up. I still hadn't deduced: was there value, in this sorrow?

The occasional midday Triscuit-and-hummus snack break brought family members together in the kitchen, but rarely did crackers and chickpeas segue into chats that went too far beyond the flavor of either.

Until one summer afternoon, Dad and I were both refilling waters at the same time. Maybe it was the warm breeze through the screen door that carried it, or maybe it was just plain procrastination, but something shifted. Deep in thought, Dad washed his hands for longer than the recommend twenty seconds, and then looked at me.

"So… is the point of your book that people shouldn't report?"

Dad wasn't always on the front porch, but he valiantly absorbed all the energy before, after, and around it. He lived amidst our ongoing honest, robust conversation, and though he sometimes couldn't relate, he listened. He was constantly hearing, and that mattered. And then sometimes, he was there.

Like in the middle of the day on a Tuesday in the kitchen, apparently. I choked on my water, for a beat. And then I thought.

The innate truth: the only way to actually end sexual violence is through reporting. Cops can't convict a person they don't know about. But in our current system, perpetrators aren't being convicted even when law enforcement does know.

Systems aren't perfect just because they're there. Not even close. But, as the majority of people have decided, reporting into this system isn't even "better than nothing." It's quite literally worse than nothing. Not saying anything—going unreported—helps healing, while its inverse has the potential to create more loss.

This book is not an instruction manual, but rather, an observation of that additional loss. In examining it, we come to envision a system that avoids it. We listen to why she didn't report in an effort to illuminate the conditions under which she would have.

And when the system (hopefully, eventually, finally) does account for those conditions, it's on law enforcement to make society aware. *We hear you,* they could say, *and now we're better.* It is both as simple and as groundbreaking as that.

Of course, I didn't say any of that to Dad, right then.

"No, definitely not. It's more—"

I considered the drafts waiting back in my room, about how there were so many complex issues wrapped up in them. About how, ultimately, it seemed that the root of unreported sexual violence was tied to the need for massive reforms. About how that type of change would take a while, and about how I still wasn't sure what the solution was, for now.

"—well, you'll see."

*

The suffering optimist in me flatly refused to continue believing in the systems that had let so many people down, for so long. But, in thinking about progress and its patterns, I realized:

You can't change anything without first believing in it. In its potential, at least.

Changemakers are inherently optimistic. It's a powerful perspective, one that requires more effort than pessimism does—one that creates more pain, too. But positivity reigns over any kind of reform. Belief in potential is its gospel.

The place where I'd felt the most potential ever? The front porch.

That sacred space where everything is talked about, and nothing's taboo. A place that reminds us all that not talking about darkness only makes it feel darker, and that words are like sunlight. They expose, they nurture, and then, they heal. On the front porch, there is value in healing—by extension, there is value in the suffering that comes before.

We can find the front porch anywhere, simply by gravitating to each other's arms. By unravelling our stories in places we feel secure, and letting others learn from the brave and layered "how to's" that are threaded through them. By warning them and alerting them. Without a system in place to protect us, the front porch is the best we have. It's what a person needs for healing.

Coincidentally, front-porch skills are the same skills law enforcement needs if they want to be effective. To be able to listen to a person tell a story—listen and, for a moment, just exist. To show up in that interview room as a protector of people, yes, but to show up as a person too. To maintain the fairness and unbiased vantage point that comes with being a protector, but also, to live in the compassion and imperfection that comes with being a person.

Story shows us "how to" do just about anything. Even fix a system. Law enforcement could gain a lot from sitting and listening.

Maybe it's not about any loud message leaving the front porch, after all. Maybe solutions won't come from ideas carrying down the street, mangling their way through the existing systems and bureaucracy. That's a long way for words to travel. Maybe they don't need to go anywhere.

We always knew we were doing more, here, than just twirling hair and opining. We're saving each other.

Law enforcement simply needs to come join us, between screens on secondhand couches. We're on the front porch.

There's room.

References

―――――

INTRODUCTION

Breiding, Matthew J., Sharon G. Smith, Kathleen C. Basile, Mikel L. Walters, Jieru Chen, and Melissa T. Merrick. *Prevalence and Characteristics of Sexual Violence, Stalking, and Intimate Partner Violence Victimization — National Intimate Partner and Sexual Violence Survey, United States, 2011.* Atlanta: CDC, 2014. https://www.cdc.gov/mmwr/pdf/ss/ss6308.pdf.

Human Rights Campaign. "Sexual Assault and the LGBTQ Community." Accessed February 19, 2021. https://www.hrc.org/resources/sexual-assault-and-the-lgbt-community.

Lisak, David, and Paul M. Miller, "Repeat Rape and Multiple Offending among Undetected Rapists." *Violence and Victims* 17, no. 1, (February 2002)https://time.com/wp-content/uploads/2014/09/repeat_rape.pdf.

National Sexual Violence Resource Center. "Statistics about Sexual Violence." Accessed February 19, 2021. https://www.nsvrc.org/sites/default/files/publications_nsvrc_factsheet_media-packet_statistics-about-sexual-violence_0.pdf.

RAINN (Rape, Abuse & Incest National Network). "Statistics." Accessed February 19, 2021. https://www.rainn.org/statistics#:~:text=Every%2073%20seconds%2C%20an%20American,will%20end%20up%20in%20prison.

RAINN (Rape, Abuse & Incest National Network). "The Criminal Justice System: Statistics." Accessed February 19, 2021. https://www.rainn.org/statistics/criminal-justice-system#:~:text=The%20Majority%20of%20Sexual%20Assaults,out%20of%204%20go%20unreported.&text=Members%20of%20the%20military%3A%2043,10%25%20of%20male%20victims%20reported.

The New York Times. "Read Christine Blasey Ford's Prepared Statement." *The New York Times*, September 26, 2018. https://www.nytimes.com/2018/09/26/us/politics/christine-blasey-ford-prepared-statement.html.

Trump, Donald J. (@RealDonaldTrump). "I have no doubt that, if the attack on Dr. Ford was as bad as she says, charges would have either been immediately filed with local Law Enforcement Authorities by either her or her loving parents. I ask that she bring those filings forward so that we can learn date, time, and place!" Twitter, September 21, 2018. https://twitter.com/realdonaldtrump/status/1043126336473055235. (User banned).

ALL THAT YOU'LL FIND

CBS News. "#WhyIDidntReport: Hundreds of Thousands Confide Their Stories of Rape, Abuse." *CBS This Morning*, September 24, 2018. https://www.cbsnews.com/news/whyididntreport-hundreds-of-thousands-confide-their-stories-of-rape-abuse/.

Chondoma, Lerato (@blkfaerie). "#WhyIDidntReport, Because I was a party girl at university, Because I went home with him, Because I thought everyone would say I asked for it, Because I thought this was just what happened when you partied too hard, Because I thought no one would believe me, I thought I deserved it." Twitter. September 22, 2018. https://twitter.com/blkfaerie/status/1043354098496491520.

Leong, Caitlyn (@caitlyn_leong). "Moving forward felt more important than justice. #WhyIDidntReport." Twitter. September 22, 2018, 1:14p.m. https://twitter.com/caitlyn_leong/status/1043549225584402432.

Miller, Chanel. *Know My Name*. New York: Viking Press, 2019.

Lisak, David, and Paul M. Miller. "Repeat Rape and Multiple Offending among Undetected Rapists." *Violence and Victims* 17, no. 1, (February 2002)https://time.com/wp-content/uploads/2014/09/repeat_rape.pdf.

Relman, Eliza. "The 26 Women Who Have Accused Trump of Sexual Misconduct." *Business Insider,* September 17, 2020. https://www.businessinsider.com/women-accused-trump-sexual-misconduct-list-2017-12.

Rohwein. Dr. Julie (@jirohweinn). "He was on the campus police force. I felt stupid because I'd trusted him. I knew no one would believe me. #WhyIDidntReport." Twitter. September 22, 2018, 1:14p.m. https://twitter.com/jirohwein/status/1044236866466336768.

ALL THAT YOU WON'T

Online Etymology Dictionary. s.v. "Survive (v.)." Accessed February 19, 2021. https://www.etymonline.com/word/survive.

RAINN (Rape, Abuse & Incest National Network). "Key Terms and Phrases." Accessed February 19, 2021. https://www.rainn.org/articles/key-terms-and-phrases.

"Victim or Victor?" *Random Lightbulb Moments*, January 23, 2012. https://randomlightbulbmoments.wordpress.com/2012/01/23/victim-or-victor/#:~:text=The%20words%20victim%20and%20victor,so%20diametrically%20opposed%20in%20meaning.

LAKES

60 Minutes. "Chanel Miller." Reporting by Bill Whitaker. September 22, 2019. Video. https://www.cbsnews.com/video/chanel-miller-the-full-60-minutes-report-on-the-know-my-name-author-and-brock-turner-sexual-assault-survivor-2019-09-22/#x.

Baker, Katie J. M. "Here's the Powerful Letter the Stanford Victim Read to Her Attacker." *Buzzfeed,* June 3, 2016. https://www.buzzfeednews.com/article/katiejmbaker/heres-the-powerful-letter-the-stanford-victim-read-to-her-ra.

Bice, Daniel. "Bice: Sen. Ron Johnson Suggests Christine Blasey Ford May Have 'False Memories' of Alleged Assault." *Milwaukee Journal Sentinel,* September 29, 2018. https://www.jsonline.com/story/news/investigations/daniel-bice/2018/09/29/ron-johnson-suggests-christine-blasey-ford-may-have-false-memories/1460162002/.

Brown, Emma. "California Professor, Writer of Confidential Brett Kavanaugh Letter, Speaks Out about Her Allegation of Sexual Assault." *The Washington Post,* September 16, 2018. https://www.washingtonpost.com/investigations/california-professor-writer-of-confidential-brett-kavanaugh-letter-speaks-out-about-her-allegation-of-sexual-assault/2018/09/16/46982194-b846-11e-8-94eb-3bd52dfe917b_story.html.

Cassidy, John. "The Senate Republican's Less-Than-Human Treatment of Christine Blasey Ford." *The New Yorker,* September 28, 2018. https://www.newyorker.com/news/our-columnists/the-senate-republicans-less-than-human-treatment-of-christine-blasey-ford.

Hemingway, Mollie, and Carrie Severino. "21 Reasons Not to Believe Christine Blasey Ford's Claims About Justice Kavanaugh." *The Federalist,* December 2, 2019. https://thefederalist.com/2019/12/02/21-reasons-not-to-believe-christine-blasey-fords-claims-about-justice-kavanaugh/.

"Kavanaugh hearing: Transcript." September 27, 2018, *The Washington Post.* Transcript. https://www.washingtonpost.com/news/national/wp/2018/09/27/kavanaugh-hearing-transcript/.

Miller, Chanel. *Know My Name.* New York: Viking Press, 2019.

Phelps, Jordyn. "Trump Mocks Christine Blasey Ford, Who Accused Kavanaugh of Sexual Assault." *ABC News,* October 3, 2018. https://abcnews.go.com/Politics/trump-mocks-christine-blasey-ford-ive-false-accusations/story?id=58246927.

Post Editorial Board. "Christine Blasey Ford's Lies and Other Commentary." *New York Post,* December 2, 2019. https://nypost.com/2019/12/02/christine-blasey-fords-lies-and-other-commentary/.

"Read the Letter Christine Blasey Ford Sent Accusing Brett Kavanaugh of Sexual Misconduct." CNN, September 17, 2018.https://www.cnn.com/2018/09/16/politics/blasey-ford-kavanaugh-letter-feinstein/index.html.

The New York Times. "Read Christine Blasey Ford's Prepared Statement." *The New York Times*, September 26, 2018. https://www.nytimes.com/2018/09/26/us/politics/christine-blasey-ford-prepared-statement.html.

Williamson, Elizabeth, Rebecca R. Ruiz, Emily Steel, Grace Ashford, and Steve Eder. "For Christine Blasey Ford, a Drastic Turn from a Quiet Life in Academia." *New York Times*, September 19, 2018. https://www.nytimes.com/2018/09/19/us/politics/christine-blasey-ford-brett-kavanaugh-allegations.html.

PRIVATE LIFE

Bayer, Mike. "Lauren O'Connor on 'The Coach Mike Podcast.'" *Los Angeles Times*, March 20, 2020, video, 2:23. https://www.latimes.com/iajwaznozvo-123.

Benedict, Helen. *Virgin or Vamp: How the Press Covers Sex Crimes*. New York: Oxford University Press, 1992.

Carmon, Irin, and Amelia Schonbek. "Was It Worth It?" *New York Magazine, The Cut*, September 30, 2019. https://www.thecut.com/2019/09/coming-forward-about-sexual-assault-and-what-comes-after.html.

Kantor, Jodi, and Megan Twohey. "Harvey Weinstein Paid off Sexual Harassment Accusers for Decades." *New York Times*, October 5, 2017. https://www.nytimes.com/2017/10/05/us/harvey-weinstein-harassment-allegations.html.

Kantor, Jodi, and Megan Twohey. *She Said*. New York: Penguin Press, 2019.

Lauren O'Connor's LinkedIn profile. Accessed February 19, 2021. https://www.linkedin.com/in/lauren-o-connor-ba97641a/.

Miller, Chanel. *Know My Name*. New York: Viking Press, 2019.

Neason, Alexandria, and Nausicaa Renner. "The Media Bullying of Christine Blasey Ford." Columbia Journalism Review, September 27, 2018.

O'Connor, Lauren. Interview by Amy Goodman. *Democracy Now!* January 29, 2019. https://www.democracynow.org/2019/1/29/exclusive_ex_harvey_weinstein_employee_breaks.

TO WORK, GROW, AND BE RESPECTED

Carmon, Irin, and Amelia Schonbek. "Was It Worth It?" *New York Magazine, The Cut*, September 30, 2019. https://www.thecut.com/2019/09/coming-forward-about-sexual-assault-and-what-comes-after.html.

Garrett, Olivia. Letter to Representative Bryce Edgmon and Representative Chris Tuck. March 13, 2017. https://s3.amazonaws.com/arc-wordpress-client-uploads/adn/wp-content/uploads/2017/12/08022151/Westlake.Letter.pdf.

Herz, Nathaniel, and Julia O'Malley. "Seven Aides at Alaska Capitol Say Legislator Made Unwanted Advances and Comments." *Anchorage Daily News*, December 8, 2017. https://www.adn.com/politics/alaska-legislature/2017/12/08/seven-aides-at-alaska-capitol-say-legislator-made-unwanted-advances-and-comments/.

Hopkins, Kyle. "'He Should Resign. It's That Simple.' Woman Who Says She Was Groped by Alaska Lawmaker Says Apology Is Not Enough." *KTUU*, December 8, 2017. https://www.alaskasnewssource.com/content/news/He-should-resign-Its-that-simple-Woman-who-says-she-was-groped-by-Alaska-lawmaker-says-apology-is-not-enough-462916373.html.

GUILT AND SPACES

Active Collective. "Why Attend." Accessed February 19, 2021. https:// activewearcollective.com/why-attend/.

Adam McKay, dir. *Step Brothers*. 2000. Los Angeles, CA: Sony Pictures Releasing, 2008. Blu-ray Disc, 1080p HD.

Albergotti, Reed. "Silicon Valley Women Tell of VC's Unwanted Advances." *The Information*, June 22, 2017. https://www.theinformation.com/articles/silicon-valley-women-tell-of-vcs-unwanted-advances.

Axios. "Talk of Tech: Women Reveal Silicon Valley's Sexism." *Axios*, July 1, 2017. https://www.axios.com/talk-of-tech-women-reveal-silicon-valleys-sexism-2451494779.html.

Benner, Katie. "Women in Tech Speak Frankly on Culture of Harassment." *The New York Times*, June 30, 2017. https://www.nytimes.com/2017/06/30/technology/women-entrepreneurs-speak-out-sexual-harassment.html.

Carmon, Irin, and Amelia Schonbek. "Was It Worth It?" *New York Magazine, The Cut*, September 30, 2019. https://www.thecut.com/2019/09/coming-forward-about-sexual-assault-and-what-comes-after.html.

Lindsay Meyer's LinkedIn Profile. Accessed February 19, 2021. https://www.linkedin.com/in/lindsaykmeyer/.

Mac, Ryan. "Disgraced Venture Capitalist Justin Caldbeck Threatened Legal Action against One of His Accusers." *Buzzfeed*, September 6, 2017. https://www.buzzfeednews.com/article/ryanmac/this-venture-capitalist-was-accused-of-sexual-harassment.

Peterson, Diane. "'Silence Breaker' Lindsay Meyer Talks about Harassment in High-Tech." *The Press Democrat*, March 16, 2018. https://www.pressdemocrat.com/lifestyle/8096084-181/silence-breaker-lindsay-meyer-talks?artslide=0&sba=AAS.

Zacharek, Stephanie, Eliana Dockterman, and Haley Sweetland Edwards. "The Silence Breakers." *TIME*, December 6, 2017. https://time.com/time-person-of-the-year-2017-silence-breakers/.

FAMILY MATTERS

Betancourt, Sarah. "'Cardinal Law Allowed This to Happen': Abuse Survivors on Archbishop's Death." *The Guardian*, December 21, 2017. https://www.theguardian.com/us-news/2017/dec/20/cardinal-bernard-law-death-survivors-react.

Carmon, Irin, and Amelia Schonbek. "Was It Worth It?" *New York Magazine, The Cut,* September 30, 2019. https://www.thecut.com/2019/09/coming-forward-about-sexual-assault-and-what-comes-after.html.

Miller, Mike. "The Incredible Story of Spotlight's Phil Saviano: The Child Sex Abuse Survivor Who Refused to Be Silenced by the Catholic Church." *People,* February 05, 2016. https://people.com/movies/the-incredible-story-of-spotlights-phil-saviano/.

Oscars. "'Spotlight' Wins Best Picture." March 23, 2016. Video, 03:12. https://www.youtube.com/watch?v=ZKV3TKuHm3k.

Rezendes, Michael. "Church Allowed Abuse by Priest for Years." *The Boston Globe,* January 6, 2002. https://www.bostonglobe.com/news/special-reports/2002/01/06/church-allowed-abuse-priest-for-years/cSHfGkTIrAT25qKGvBuDNM/story.html.

BIGGER OR SMALLER

Battaglio, Stephen. "New York Attorney General's Office Questioned NBC News Employees on Sexual Harassment." *Los Angeles Times,* May 5, 2020. https://www.latimes.com/entertainment-arts/business/story/2020-05-05/new-york-attorney-general-questions-nbc-news-employees-sexual-harassment-lauer.

Carmon, Irin, and Amelia Schonbek. "Was It Worth It?" *New York Magazine, The Cut,* September 30, 2019. https://www.thecut.com/2019/09/coming-forward-about-sexual-assault-and-what-comes-after.html.

de Moraes, Lisa. "NBC News Faces Skepticism in Remedying in-House Sexual Harassment." *Deadline,* April 27, 2018. https://deadline.com/2018/04/tom-brokaw-denies-linda-vester-claims-sexual-harassment-washington-post-variety-1202378351/#!.

Ellison, Sarah. "NBC News Faces Skepticism in Remedying in-House Sexual Harassment." *The Washington Post,* April 26, 2018. https://www.washingtonpost.com/lifestyle/style/nbc-news-faces-skepticism-in-remedying-in-house-sexual-harassment/2018/04/26/7fa8a666-4979-11e8-8b5a-3b1697adcc2a_story.html.

Kilkenny, Katie. "Rachel Maddow, Andrea Mitchell Back Tom Brokaw in Letter Signed by 64 Insiders." *The Hollywood Reporter,* April 27, 2018. https://www.hollywoodreporter.com/news/rachel-maddow-andrea-mitchell-voice-support-tom-brokaw-letter-1106645.

Merriam-Webster Online. Academic ed. s.v. "safety." Accessed February 19, 2021. https://www.merriam-webster.com/dictionary/safety.

Vester, Linda. "Why I Revealed That Tom Brokaw Harassed Me." *The Washington Post,* May 9, 2018. https://www.washingtonpost.com/opinions/why-i-revealed-that-tom-brokaw-harassed-me/2018/05/09/748f3222-530b-11e8-abd8-265bd07a9859_story.html?noredirect=on.

Wagmeister, Elizabeth, and Ramin Setoodeh. "Matt Lauer Accused of Sexual Harassment by Multiple Women (Exclusive)." *Variety,* November 29, 2017. https://variety.com/2017/biz/news/matt-lauer-accused-sexual-harassment-multiple-women-1202625959/.

Wagmeister, Elizabeth, and Ramin Setoodeh "Tom Brokaw Accused of Sexual Harassment by Former NBC Anchor (Exclusive Video)." *Variety,* April 26, 2018. https://variety.com/2018/tv/news/tom-brokaw-sexual-harassment-nbc-news-correspondent-1202789627/.

IN PURSUIT OF A FAIR OUTCOME

Battaglia, Andy. "Will Emma Sulkowicz's Protest Mattress Wind up in a Museum?" *Vulture,* May 28, 2015. https://www.vulture.com/2015/05/does-sulkowiczs-mattress-belong-in-a-museum.html.

Bernard, Joan Kelly. "ELLE's E. Jean Carroll Dishes Out Sassy but Sane Advice." *News & Record,* January 25, 2015. https://greensboro.com/elle-s-e-jean-carroll-dishes-out-sassy-but-sane/article_d491c6c6-68d0-5bbf-baab-1261bc52cbcf.html.

Bogler, Emma. "Frustrated by Columbia's Inaction, Student Reports Sexual Assault to Police." *Columbia Spectator,* December 28, 2016. https://www.columbiaspectator.com/news/2014/05/16/frustrated-columbias-inaction-student-reports-sexual-assault-police/.

Bogler, Emma. "Students File Federal Complaint against Columbia, Alleging Title IX, Title II, Clery Act Violations." *Columbia Spectator,* April 24, 2014. https://web.archive.org/web/20140428070027/http://www.columbiaspectator.com/news/2014/04/24/students-file-federal-complaint-against-columbia-alleging-title-ix-title-ii-clery.

Carroll, E. Jean (@ejeancarroll1). "I am suing the President of the United States for Defamation. I am filing not just for me but for every woman who's been pinched, prodded, cornered, felt up, pushed against the wall, grabbed, groped, assaulted, and had spoken up only to be shamed, demeaned, disgraced, passed over for promotion, fired and forgotten. I am filing this suit because Donald Trump is not above the law! This photo was taken by @gievesanderson for @elleusa." Instagram photo, November 4, 2019. https://www.instagram.com/p/B4dAFoDnkyx/.

Carroll, E. Jean. "Ask E. Jean: January 2007." *ELLE,* December 12, 2006. https://www.elle.com/life-love/ask-e-jean/q-and-a/a9199/ask-e-jean-january-2007-19308/.

Carroll, E. Jean. "Ask E. Jean: My Boyfriend and I Keep Getting into the Same Fight about Feminism." *ELLE,* June 16, 2016. https://www.elle.com/life-love/ask-e-jean/advice/a37119/ask-e-jean-boyfriend-less-feminist/.

Carroll, E. Jean. "Ask E. Jean: The Evolution of Wooing." *ELLE,* August 26, 2013. https://www.elle.com/life-love/ask-e-jean/q-and-a/a13757/e-jean-20-years-dating/.

Carroll, E. Jean. "Hideous Men Donald Trump Assaulted Me in a Bergdorf Goodman Dressing Room 23 Years Ago. But He's Not Alone on the List of Awful Men in My Life." *The Cut,* June 21, 2019. https://www.thecut.com/2019/06/donald-trump-assault-e-jean-carroll-other-hideous-men.html.

CBS NY. "Sen. Kirsten Gillibrand Seeks Funds to Fight College Campus Sex Assaults." *CBSN NY,* April 2, 2014. https://newyork.cbslocal.com/2014/04/07/sen-kirsten-gillibrand-seeks-funds-to-fight-college-campus-sex-assaults/.

Fuller, Bonnie. "E. Jean Carroll: 5 Things on Writer Facing off with Justice Dept. over Her Trump Rape Charge." *Hollywood Life by Bonnie Fuller*, September 8, 2020. https://hollywoodlife.com/feature/who-is-e-jean-carroll-3646042/.

Gentleman, Amelia. "Prosecuting Sexual Assault: 'Raped All over Again.'" *The Guardian*, April 13, 2013. https://www.theguardian.com/society/2013/apr/13/rape-sexual-assault-frances-andrade-court.

Lah, Kyung. "Alabama Man Won't Serve Prison Time for Raping 14-Year-Old." *CNN*, September 26, 2013. https://www.cnn.com/2013/09/26/us/montana-teacher-rape/index.html.

Morris, Nigel. "100,000 Assaults. 1,000 Rapists Sentenced. Shockingly Low Conviction Rates Revealed." *The Independent*, January 10, 2013. https://www.independent.co.uk/news/uk/crime/100000-assaults-1000-rapists-sentenced-shockingly-low-conviction-rates-revealed-8446058.html.

New York Magazine. "E. Jean Carroll on the Aftermath of Publishing Her Story." June 24, 2019. Video, 05:09. https://www.youtube.com/watch?v=zi4DSmdUdng.

Palmeri, Tara. "Columbia Drops Ball on Jock 'Rapist' Probe: Students." *New York Post*, December 11, 2013. https://nypost.com/2013/12/11/co-eds-rip-columbia-over-athlete-rape-probes/.

RAINN (Rape, Abuse & Incest National Network). "Statistics." Accessed February 19, 2021. https://www.rainn.org/statistics#:~:text=Every%2073%20seconds%2C%20an%20American,will%20end%20up%20in%20prison.

Redden, Molly. "Alabama Man Won't Serve Prison Time for Raping 14-Year-Old." *Mother Jones*, November 15, 2013. https://www.motherjones.com/politics/2013/11/alabama-man-no-prison-time-raping-teenager/.

Robbins, Christopher. "Spurned by Columbia, Student Says NYPD Mistreated Her While Reporting Rape." *Gothamist*, May 18, 2014. http://gothamist.com/2014/05/18/spurned_by_columbia_student_says_ny.php.

Rosman, Katherine, and Jessica Bennett. "What Happened between E. Jean Carroll and ELLE Magazine?" *The New York Times*, February 21, 2020. https://www.nytimes.com/2020/02/21/style/ejean-carroll-fired-elle.html#:~:text=Carroll%20accuses%20Donald%20Trump%20of,news%20outlets%20around%20the%20world.&text=Carroll%2C%20calling%20oher%20a%20liar.

Smith, Roberta. "In a Mattress, a Lever for Art and Political Protest." *The New York Times*, September 21, 2014. https://www.nytimes.com/2014/09/22/arts/design/in-a-mattress-a-fulcrum-of-art-and-political-protest.html.

Taub, Amanda. "Columbia's Response to Campus Rape Is 'Prolonged, Degrading, and Ultimately Fruitless'." *Vox*, October 3, 2014. https://www.vox.com/2014/10/3/6900179/parents-of-columbia-rape-victim-say-campus-justice-was-prolonged.

TV Worth Watching. "This Day in History: July 4, 2012." Accessed February 19, 2021. http://www.tvworthwatching.com/post/THISDAYINTVHISTORY201207-4.aspx.

Zawadi, Lucy. "E Jean Carroll Biography: Age, Trump Lawsuit, Is She Married?" *Legit,* September 2020. https://www.legit.ng/1365565-e-jean-carroll-biography-age-trump-lawsuit-married.html.

STOP THE BLEEDING

"How Wounds Heal." Medicine Plus, accessed February 19, 2021. https://medlineplus.gov/ency/patientinstructions/000741.htm.

Technology, Entertainment, Design. "The Power of Vulnerability | Brené Brown." January 3, 2011, video. https://www.youtube.com/watch?v=iCvmsMzlF70.

Whittington, Brian. "Understanding the 3 Phases of Muscle Healing." *Athletico Physical Therapy,* March 27, 2017. https://www.athletico.com/2017/03/27/understanding-the-3-phases-of-muscle-healing/.

NOTHING IS FOR EVERYONE

C-Span. "Sexual Assault on College Campuses." June 23, 2014, video. https://www.c-span.org/video/?320111-1/sexual-assault-college-campuses.

Homepage. 1in6. Accessed March 5, 2021. https://1in6.org/.

Lehman, Chris. "Report: Oregon Has Very High Rate of Female Sexual Assault." *OPB,* September 21, 2016. https://www.opb.org/news/article/sexual-assault-high-rate-oregon-women-girls-report/.

Lisak, David, and Paul M. Miller. "Repeat Rape and Multiple Offending among Undetected Rapists." *Violence and Victims* 17, no. 1, (February 2002)https://time.com/wp-content/uploads/2014/09/repeat_rape.pdf.

Morad, Renee. "Liz Plank: Why Traditional Masculinity Remains a Barrier for Us All." *NBC News, Know Your Value.* January 8, 2021. https://www.nbcnews.com/know-your-value/feature/liz-plank-why-traditional-masculinity-remains-barrier-us-all-ncna1253380.

You Have Options Program. "About Us." Accessed February 19, 2021. https://www.reportingoptions.org/about-us/.

You Have Options Program. "Explore Your Options." Accessed February 19, 2021. https://www.reportingoptions.org/explore-your-options/.

YOU'RE INVITED

Axelrod, Julie. "The 5 Stages of Grief & Loss." *Psych Central,* May 17, 2016. https://psychcentral.com/lib/the-5-stages-of-loss-and-grief#5.

Kessler, David. *Finding Meaning: The Sixth Stage of Grief.* New York. Scribner, 2019.

Gratitude

———

Word on the street is that writing a book is a horrible, lonely endeavor. These people made it feel like the opposite.

To the women and men who appear in the pages before this, thank you for your trust, your truth, and your belief in the power of shared story.

To the original front porch, who held this new conversation with me over emails and hours-long phone calls; Mom, Kendall, Daven, Bobbie, Holly, and Grammie, thanks for your love, humor, and for bringing sunlight to this topic.

To Dad, for asking the hard questions, and to Grandpa Bliss, who told me that life is for finding what you love and using it to help others. And to Dave, thank you doesn't even begin to cover it.

To the Californian front porch that left the light on: Amy, Haley, and Fallon. Thanks for feeling it all with me. Blues in the verse, gospel in the chorus (or something like that).

To Pop and Kip, Matt and Jess, Janine and Andy, Kristina and Mikey, Joe and Lynn, and Brett and Mitch. I'm happy life stuck us together.

To Joe, Ashley, Kristen, Brynn, Megan C., Ally, and Lauren, who helped me live the first draft of this story. To Dev,

Jillian, Kati, Francesca, and Tyler, who helped me believe a book was possible, and to Elina, Steph, Jaclyn, Eric, Bill, and Cortni, who helped me see exactly how.

To Caroline, Kiki, Ben, Lee, Justin, and Billy: lucky to keep growing up with you. Thanks for double-checking my math in more ways than one.

To Dak and A.P., thank you for thinking so deeply and devoting yourself to this mission.

To Jane Regan (etc.), Fran Shea, Jeff Beale, Grant Place, Ryan Thurston, Eric Proctor, and Sharon Katzman, thanks for being educators in more ways than one.

And to the following, who supported these stories before some of them were even written:

Adriana Rabunski, Andrea Costa, Angela Taylor, Anne Marie Arsenault, Austin Edwards, Aviana Vergnetti, Becky Lillie, Caitlin Flanagan, Celene Beth Calderon, Charene Clark, Charon Burns, Chelsey Lustig, Chrissy Gerardi, Christine Adornetto, Cindy O'Malley, Claire Christine Sargenti, Dan Gaffey, Donna Jutila, Elisabeth Story, Elise Petersen, Fran Green, Greg Ux, Gretchen Dean, Ines Horneij, Jacob Suggs, Jane Rozzero, Jayme Ritchie, Jessica Gelbwaks, John Ricci, Jolene Hiltz, Judy Lanza, Julie Woodward, Karna Hopkins, Katy Cooke, Kendall Dunlop-Korsness, Laura Shea, Lorraine Swintek, MacKenzie Bachry, Maggie Morris, Marla Lance, Micha Sabovik, Nancy Perrault, Nick Neville, Peter O'Neill, Phil DeFronzo, Ryan Lader, Shane Christian O'Connor, Shelby Cole, Simone Rodriguez, Stephanie DeLorenzo, Sue Fiscus, Susan Cohen, and Trisha Thadani.

Kaley Roberts is a writer living in Brooklyn, New York. By day, she works in documentary television. This is her first book.

9 781636 769073